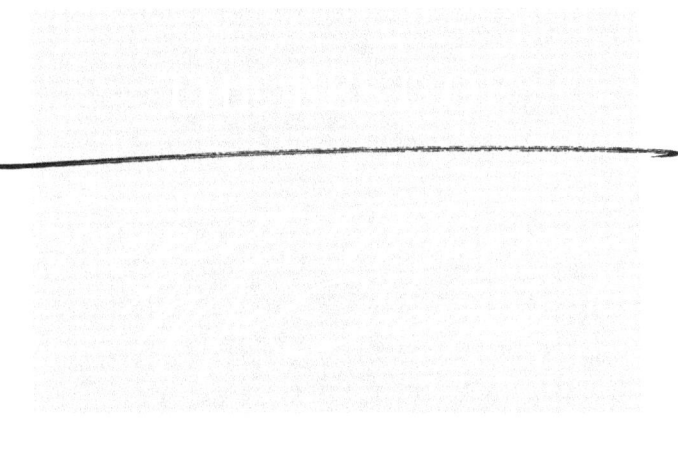

120 Daily Devotions

TO NURTURE YOUR SPIRIT AND
REFRESH YOUR SOUL

Editor's note: The selections in this book have been "gently modernized" for today's reader. Words, phrases, and sentence structure have been updated for readability and clarity; new chapter headings and Scripture verses have been combined with excerpts from Robert Murray McCheyne's text. Every effort has been made to preserve the integrity and intent of McCheyne's original writings. Reflection questions at the end of each reading have been included to aid in personal exploration and group discussion.

The Best of Robert Murray McCheyne
ISBN: 979-8-88898-156-6 - *Paperback*
ISBN: 979-8-88898-157-3 - *Hardcover*
ISBN: 979-8-88898-158-0 - *Ebook*

Copyright © 2024 by Honor Books
Racine, WI

Edited and complied by Stephen W. Sorenson.
Cover design by Faille Schmitz.

ABOUT ROBERT MURRAY MCCHEYNE

*Short Life,
Big Influence*

The Scottish pastor and theologian Robert Murray McCheyne lived only three decades (1813-1843), but he accomplished great things in that brief span. As one historian noted, "Few men have had the impact in a long lifetime that Robert Murray McCheyne had in his thirty years."

Born in Edinburgh to a middle-class family, McCheyne demonstrated early on the keen intellect that would serve him well in school and ministry during the years ahead. At the age of four, he taught himself the Greek alphabet and later committed lengthy Scripture passages to memory. He entered high school in his eighth year and then, in 1827, entered the University of Edinburgh. There, he showed exceptional facility with language, earning recognition and winning awards for original poetry. It was during his last year at the university that his older brother David died, an event that McCheyne said had a profound effect on him and served as a turning point in his spiritual life.

A few months after his brother's death, McCheyne entered the divinity school at the University of Edinburgh, where he studied under Professor Thomas

Chalmers, who greatly influenced his life and ministry aims. At Chalmers' urging, his protege joined the Missionary Association, which emphasized care for the poor and overseas missions. Both causes became essential aspects of McCheyne's later ministry.

Upon graduation, McCheyne was appointed assistant to the Rev. John Bonar of Larbert. So active was McCheyne in his new role that his health, which had never been robust, broke down. Still, his reputation as a dynamic preacher had grown, and he was called to pastor St. Peter's Church, Dundee, in 1836. He was twenty-three years old. The congregation, which numbered 1,100, was comprised mostly of working-class people. Some questioned whether the youthful and erudite McCheyne could succeed among the largely lower-class and uneducated community. But with his winsome personality, practical teaching style, and innovative ideas, he was more than up to the challenge. He started numerous programs—Bible-study classes, service projects to aid the poor, evangelistic outreaches—and St. Peter's flourished. The church grew in both membership and spiritual fervor.

Drawing on his knowledge of music, McCheyne was one of the first Scottish ministers to take an active role in changing and improving congregational services, adding more emphasis on praise and worship. His services were said to be much more compelling and lively than most others at that time. In addition to his pastoral responsibilities, he wrote numerous hymns—including "When This Passing World Is Done" and "I Am a Debtor"—that are still used in Scottish churches and elsewhere. Given all this activity, it is not surprising that McCheyne again compromised his health and was forced to take a leave of absence.

In 1839, the general assembly of the Church of Scotland decided to appoint a committee to study and suggest ways to evangelize Jews. Because of McCheyne's passion for missions work, he was appointed to the commission. He and a small delegation set sail and weeks later arrived in Palestine to begin collecting information. During the course of their six-month journey—arduous at that time, to say the least—reports were sent home and published in the national press. A complete record of the journey was coauthored by McCheyne and Andrew Bonar, his close friend and colleague. Published in 1842, Narrative of a *Mission of Inquiry to the Jews* was widely read and influential.

While in the Middle East, McCheyne had prayed fervently for his congregation back home. Upon his return, he found that a revival was underway. He resumed his ministerial duties in Dundee with renewed vigor and oversaw continued growth of his church. In 1842, he visited the north of England on an evangelistic crusade and made similar journeys to London and Aberdeenshire.

When asked about the success of his various ministry endeavors, McCheyne cited his devotional life. He made prayer, meditation, and Bible study the basis for all he did. Each day, he would rise early for two hours of meditation and prayer, including an hour devoted to Jewish people. On Sundays, he would spend six hours in prayer and devotional reading. He felt so strongly about private and family worship that he devised a yearly calendar to encourage people to read the Old Testament once and the New Testament and Psalms twice. This calendar still enjoys widespread use today.

In March of 1843, while visiting parishioners in an outlying area, McCheyne contracted typhus. After two weeks of illness, and despite St. Peter's being full every night with praying people, he passed away. Having never married, he left no immediate family—but he left an extensive number of "Christian family members" and fellow believers. In fact, more than six thousand people attended his funeral. Soon after his death, Andrew Bonar compiled *The Memoir and Remains of Robert Murray McCheyne,* a collection of sermons, lessons, and letters. This book, widely regarded as a devotional and spiritual classic, has sold hundreds of thousands of copies. If not for Bonar's foresight in undertaking the compilation, much of McCheyne's material likely would have been lost forever.

Long after his death, he was continually referred to as "the saintly McCheyne." He may have "sowed" for only a short time, but his devout life and vibrant ministry have continued to reap fruit many decades after his passing. McCheyne's brief life surely exemplified the words he so often repeated: "Live so as to be missed."

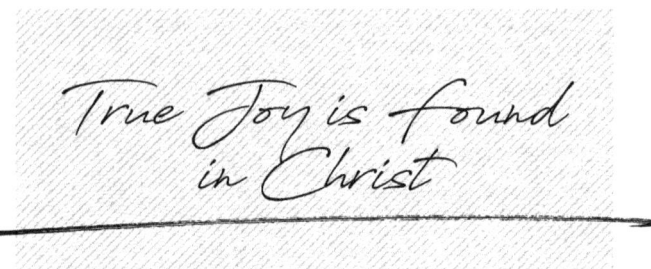

True Joy is found in Christ

"In Your presence is fullness of joy; at Your right hand are pleasures forevermore."

Psalm 16:11

Some people think there is no joy in religion, that it is a gloomy thing. When a young person becomes a Christian, his unbelieving friends say, "Now he must bid farewell to pleasure, farewell to the joys of youth, farewell to a merry heart. He must exchange these pleasures for reading the Bible and dry sermon books, for a life of continual austerity and deprivation."

This is what the world says. Ah, let God be true, and every man a liar. Be not deceived, my friends. The world has many sensual and sinful delights—the delights of eating and drinking, revelry and extravagance. No man of wisdom will deny that these things are delightful to their natural heart. But, oh, they vanish in an instant and lead to destruction.

To sit down under the shadow of Christ, wearied with God's burning anger, wearied with seeking momentary pleasures, at last to find rest under the shadow of Christ, ah, this is great delight. Lord, evermore may I sit under this shadow! Lord, evermore may I he filled with this joy!

Reflection

In what or whom
are you finding your
delights?

Are you on the
"path of life" or are
you being
sidetracked by the
world's fleeting
pleasures?

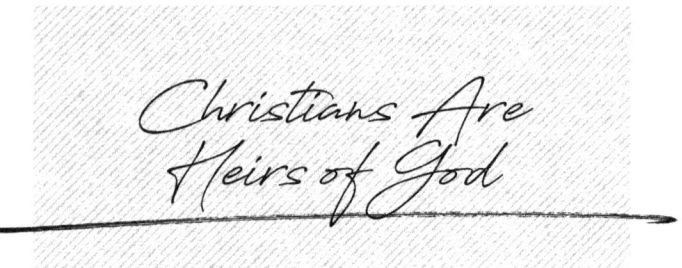

Christians Are Heirs of God

"God sent forth His Son . . . that we might
receive the adoption as sons . . . and if a son,
then an heir of God through Christ."

Galatians 4:4–5, 7

Before Jesus went up to heaven, He said, "I go to My Father" (John 14:12). Oh, it was a blessed exchange when He left the frowns and curses of this world for the embrace of His Fathers arms, when He left the thorny crown for a crown of glory, when He came from under the wrath of God into the fatherly love of God.

Such is your change, you who believe in Jesus. You have fellowship with the Son; you share in His adoption. He says, "I am ascending to My Father and your Father" (John 20:17). God is as much your Father as He is Christ's Father, your God as Christs God. Oh what a change, for an heir of hell to become an heir of God and joint heir with Christ, to inherit God, to have a son's interest in God!

Eternity alone will teach you all that is in the phrase "heir of God."

Reflection

What does it mean to you, as a believer, to be called an "heir of God"?

What do you think it'll be like when you meet God face-to-face?

Give God the Glory

"Let not the wise man glory in his wisdom,
let not the mighty man glory in his might,
nor let the rich man glory in his riches; but
let him who glories glory in this, that he
understands and knows Me."

Jeremiah 9:23–24

You were once in darkness, but now you are in the light of the Lord. Walk as children of light. Your soul was once condemned to death, but now you have been given life, and life eternal. See who did it, and give Him the praise. It is the Lord. God gave Christ to he the light to your soul. Give Him, and Him alone, the glory. "My glory I will not give to another" (Isa. 42:8).

Do not give the praise to yourself. Do not say, "My own wisdom or prayers have gotten me this." It was all undeserved mercy to the chief of sinners.

Plead with God to fulfill His word, that Christ may be a light to the nations. It is as easy with God to make Christ shine on many souls as on one. Give Him no rest until He pours down the Holy Spirit on all our families, until there is a great turning toward Jesus and rejoicing in Him. Take Your own glory, O Lord. Give it to no other.

Reflection

In what ways do you give God glory? What specifically can you praise Him for today?

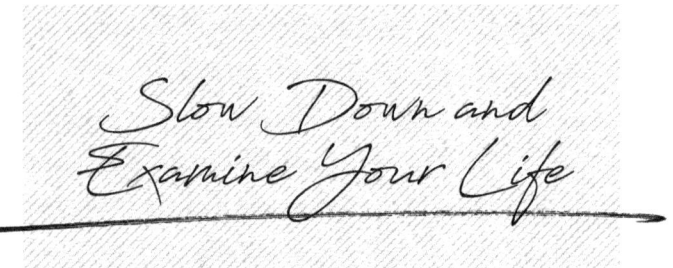

Slow Down and Examine Your Life

"Thus says the Lord of hosts: 'Consider your ways!'"

Haggai 1:5

When a traveler passes rapidly through a country, the eye has no time to rest on the different objects in that country. So when he comes to the end of his journey, no distinct impressions have been made on his mind. He has only a confused notion of the country through which he has traveled.

This explains how it is that death, judgment, and eternity make so little impression on most men's minds. Most people never stop to think, but hurry on through life and find themselves in eternity before they have asked, "What must I do to be saved?" More souls are lost through want of consideration than in any other way. The reason why men are not awakened and made anxious concerning their souls is that the Devil never gives them time to consider. Therefore, God cries, "Stop, poor sinner, stop and think. Consider your ways."

In the same way, the Devil tries to make the children of God doubt if there is a Providence. He hurries them away to the shop and market. "Lose no time," he says, "but make money." Therefore, Jesus says, "Look at the birds of the air, for they neither sow nor reap nor gather into barns . . . Consider the lilies of the field, how they grow: they neither toil nor spin" (Matt, 6:26, 28).

The Devil tries to make the children of God live uncomfortable and unholy lives. He beguiles them away from simply looking to Jesus; he hurries them away to look at a thousand other things, as he led Peter, walking on the sea, to look at the waves. But God says, "Look here. Look unto me, and be saved. Run your race, looking unto Jesus only. Stop filling your days with haste and endless activity. Let Christ give you rest and fullness of life."

Reflection

How often do you reflect on your spiritual journey?
Ask God to show you any areas in which you especially need to consider your ways and focus more on Him.

God Never Forgets You

"Lo, I am with you always, even to the end of the age."

Matthew 28:20

The children of God often think their God has forgotten them. When they fall into sin and darkness, they feel cut off from Him, as if His mercies were gone forever. But learn here that God never forgets the soul that is in Christ Jesus.

So it was with Moses in the land of Midian. For forty years, he thought God had forgotten His people. Moses wandered as a shepherd in the wilderness for forty years, sad and desolate. But had God really forgotten His people? No, He appeared in a flaming fire in a bush and said, "I have surely seen the oppression of My people who are in Egypt, and have heard their cry because of their taskmasters, for I know their sorrows" (Ex. 3:7).

The Lord cannot forget you. If you stood before God in your own righteousness, then I see how you might be separated from His love and care. But you stand before Him in Christ, and Christ is the same yesterday, today, and forever. You will be held in everlasting remembrance. The world may forget you, your friends may forget you; this is a forgetting world. You may not have a tombstone over your grave, but God will not forget you.

Reflection

Have you ever felt
abandoned by God,
that He has
forgotten you?

What were the
circumstances?

How can you be
assured that God is
with you always?

During Temptation, Draw Closer to Christ

"The weapons of our warfare are not carnal
but mighty in God for pulling down
strongholds . . . bringing every thought into
captivity to the obedience of Christ."

2 Corinthians 10:4-5

All of you have faced temptation, times of conflict between your natural conscience and the law of Clod. But that is not the contest in the believer's bosom. It is warfare between the Spirit of God in the heart and the old man with his deeds. If any of you are groaning under this warfare, learn to be humbled by it, but not discouraged. It is intended to make you lie in the dust and feel acutely your need for Christs power and forgiveness. Even after you have received the Holy Spirit, you are still prone to wander and leave the God who rescued you.

Let this make you lie low. Let this teach you your need of Jesus. You need the blood of Jesus as much now as at first. You never can stand before God in yourself. You must go again and again to be washed. Even on your thing bed, you must hide under Jehovah, our righteousness. You must also lean on Jesus. He alone can overcome the sin in you. Draw nearer and nearer to Him every day.

Don't be discouraged. Jesus is willing to be a Savior to such as you. He is able to save you to the uttermost. Do you think your case is too bad for Christ to save?

Everyone whom Christ saves had just such a heart as you. Fight the good fight of faith; lay hold of eternal life. Take up the resolution of Edwards: "Never to give over, nor in the least to slacken, my fight with my corruptions, however, unsuccessful I may be."

Reflection

What, specifically, does it mean to "draw closer to Christ" during times of temptation? How can you access His power and strength?

Jesus Will Satisfy Your Thirst

"I will pour water on him who is thirsty."

Isaiah 44:3

Often people have spent a long time under God's awakening hand. God has led them into trouble, but not into peace. He has taken them down into the wilderness, and there they wander about in search of refreshing waters, but they find none. They wander from mountain to hill seeking rest. Finding none, they go from well to well, seeking a drop of water to cool their tongues.

The whole Bible shows that God has a peculiar tenderness for those who are thirsty. Christ, who is the express image of God, had a peculiar tenderness for them: "Come to Me, all you who labor and are heavy laden, and I will give you rest . . . If anyone thirsts, let him come to Me and drink" (Matt. 11:28; John 7:37). Many of His cures were intended to win the hearts of these burdened souls. The woman who had spent all she had on other physicians and still found no cure, no sooner touched the hem of His garment than she was made whole. Another was bowed down eighteen years; but Jesus laid His hands on her and immediately she was made straight.

Wean Christian, this is Jesus, who satisfies and soothes.

This is what He wants to do for you: "I will pour water on him who is thirsty." Only believe that He is willing and able, and it will be done. Learn that it must come from His hand. In vain you go to other physicians. You will he no better, but rather worse. Wait on Him; kneel and worship Him, saying, "Lord, help me."

Reflection

What does it mean that God wall "pour water on him who is thirsty"?
In what ways does God satisfy our thirst?

Worshipping Together

"Let us consider one another in order to stir
up love and good works, not forsaking the
assembling of ourselves together, as is the
manner of some."

Hebrews 10:24-25

W hen you are weeping beside the chiseled monument of a departed friend, you don't wonder that the careless crowd passes by without a tear. They did not know the virtues of your departed friend. They do not know the fragrance of his memory. Likewise, the world cares not for the house of prayer, the sprinkled water, the broken bread, and the poured-out wine because they never knew the excellence of Jesus.

But with believers, it is quite different. You have been divinely taught your need of Jesus, and therefore you delight to hear Christ preached. You have seen the beauty of Christ crucified, therefore you love the place where He is evidently set forth. You love the very name of Jesus; it is like ointment poured forth. Therefore, you could join forever in the melody of His praises. The Sabbath day, of which you once said, "What a weariness this is" and "When will it be over, so w'e can do other things?" is now a delight and honorable, the sweetest day of all the seven.

Reflection

How has your view of the church, and the time you spend with other believers, changed as you have grown in your faith?

Why are so many people today unwilling to have much, or anything, to do with the church?

Jesus Understands Our Pain

"When He saw the multitudes, He was moved
with compassion for them."

Matthew 9:36

When you are in full health, if you hear of some sick person you are a little affected. But if you go and see, if you enter in with quiet step and see the pale face, the languid eye, and the heaving breast, then the eye affects the heart and your compassion flows like a mighty river. This is humanity; this is the way with man; this was the way with Christ.

Once they brought Him to the grave of a dearly loved friend. They said, "Come and see." What happened? "Jesus wept" (John 11:34-35). In all your afflictions. He is afflicted. For He is not a high priest who cannot be touched with a feeling of your infirmities, but was in all points tempted like we are, yet didn't sin. Some of you have little children pained and tossing in fever. Jesus pities them, for He was once a little child.

Oh, believer, you know the pains of weariness, hunger, thirst, and poverty. Tell these things to Jesus because He knew them too. You know the pains of inward heaviness, of a drooping heart, exceeding sorrow even unto death—of the hidden face of God. Jesus knew them too.

Reflection

Which difficulties are you, or a loved one, facing right now?

Tell Jesus about them, and ask for His will to be done.

He understands what you are facing and desires our trust.

The Blessings of Walking with God

"Be still, and know that I am God."

Psalm 46:10

Come into communion with God; daily walk with Him. Enoch walked with God. Once Adam walked with God in paradise as easily as you may walk from one room to another. He talked with Him concerning his judgments.

Oh, come to your God, redeemed and forgiven soul. Acquaint yourself with God and be at peace. Come to Him; do not rest short of Him. You think it is a great thing to know a lively Christian. Oil, how infinitely better it is to know God. It is your infinite blessedness. You will gain more knowledge in one hour with God than in all your life spent with man. You will get more holiness from immediately conversing with God than from all other means of grace put together.

Reflection

Looking back on the past week, how much time did you spend getting to know God better?

What are some ways you might develop a closer walk with Him?

The Spirit's Ongoing Work

"The water that I shall give him will become
in him a fountain of water springing up into
everlasting life."

John 4:14

I t appears to me that few Christians realize that this river is flowing after them. Oh, what inexpressible love and grace there is in this work of the Spirit. Is any one of you weak, faint, and ready to perish under a wicked heart and raging lusts? Or, have you got a thorn in the flesh—a messenger of Satan to buffet you—and are you driven to pray that it may be taken from you?

See here the answer to your prayer: a river of living water that flows from Christ. There is enough here for all your wants. "My grace is sufficient for you, for My strength is made perfect in weakness" (2 Cor. 12:9). Some of you are afraid of the future. You fear some approaching temptation. You fear some coming contest. See here that the river flows after you; the Spirit will abide with you forever. Oh, what love is here! Regardless of all your sinfulness and weakness and unbelief, still He abides with you, and will forever. He is "a fountain of water springing up into everlasting life." Love the Spirit, then, who so loves you.

Reflection

Do you sense the
Spirits presence and
help in your life?
Why is God's
strength made
perfect in our
weakness?

Follow the One True Christ

As a traveler prefers an apple tree to every other tree of the woods because it provides both shelter and nourishing food, so the believer prefers Christ to all other saviors. When a man is traveling in eastern countries, he is often prone to drop down under the sun's burning rays. It is a great relief when he comes to the woods. But if the traveler is hungry and faint for lack of food, he will not be content with any tree of the wood, but will select a fruit tree, under which he may sit down and find nourishment as well as shade. So it is with the soul awakened by God. The soul that is taught by God seeks for a complete Savior. The apple tree is revealed to the soul. The hungry soul chooses that evermore. He needs to be saved from hell and nourished for heaven. "Like an apple tree among the trees of the woods, so is my beloved among the sons" (Song 2:3).

Awakened souls, remember that you must not sit down under every tree that offers itself. "Take heed that no one deceives you. For many will come in My name, saying, 'I am the Christ,' and will deceive many" (Matt. 24:4-5). There are many ways of saving peace when there is no peace. You will be tempted to find peace in the world, in self-repentance, in self-reformation. Remember, choose a tree that will yield fruit as well as shade. Pray for an eye to discern the apple tree. There is no rest for the soul except under the branch God has made strong.

Reflection

Which "false christs" are hiring people today?

What can you do to prepare yourself to deal with them in God's strength and wisdom?

God Causes Growth

"I am the true vine, and My Father is the
vinedresser. Every branch in Me that does
not bear fruit He takes away; and every
branch that bears fruit He prunes, that it may
bear more fruit."

John 15:1-2

J ohn experienced many wonderful dealings of
God; he experienced many pruning of the Father.
He was a fruitful branch, and the Father pruned
him that he might bring forth more fruit. When he was
very old, he was banished to Patmos, an island in the
Aegean Sea and, it is supposed, was made a slave in the
mines there. He was a companion in tribulation, but he
had many sweet shillings of the Fathers love. He had
sweet revelations of Christ during his affliction, and he
was joyfully delivered out of all his troubles.

He experienced peculiarly the fatherly dealings of
God. And so may you, believer. Look where John looked,
believe as John believed, and, like him, you will find that
you have a Father in heaven who will care for you, who
will correct you in measure. He will preserve you and
continue to work in you until His heavenly kingdom.

Reflection

In what ways has
God "pruned" you
to cause growth?

How have you
grown spiritually in
the past year?

Holiness Sets Us Apart

"Blessed be the God and Father of our Lord
Jesus Christ, who has blessed us with every
spiritual blessing in the heavenly places in
Christ . . . that we should he holy."

Ephesians 1:3-4

There is a kind of goodness about you. You may be kind, pleasant, agreeable, good-natured, and amiable. There may be a kind of integrity about you, so that you are above stealing or King. But as long as you are in a natural state, there is not a grain of God's holiness in you. You have not a grain of that absolute hatred against all sin that God has. You have none of that flaming love for what is lovely, pure, and holy that dwells in God's heart. But the moment you believe on a manifested Christ, that moment you receive the Holy Spirit—the same Spirit who dwells in the infinite bosom of the Father dwells in you—you become partakers of God's holiness, partakers of the divine nature. You will not be as holy as God, but the stream that flows through the heart of God will be given to you. Ah, does not your heart break to be holier! Look then to Jesus, abide in Him, and you will share the same Spirit with God Himself.

Reflection

When you read the word holiness, what comes to mind?

Are you actively pursuing holiness, asking God to show you any sin in your life so you can ask for His forgiveness and pursue righteousness?

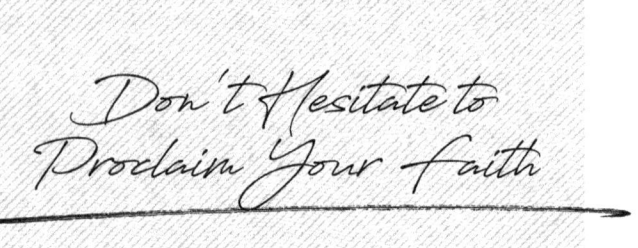

Don't Hesitate to Proclaim Your Faith

"The Spirit of the Lord God is upon Me, because the Lord has anointed Me to preach good tidings to the poor; He has sent Me to heal the brokenhearted, to proclaim liberty to the captives, and the opening of the prison to those who are bound."

Isaiah 61:1

There cannot be a secret Christian. Grace is like ointment hidden in the hand; it betrays itself. A lively Christian cannot keep silent. If you truly feel the sweetness of the cross of Christ, you will be constrained to confess Christ before other people.

Do you confess Christ in your family? Do you make it known there that you are His? Remember, you must make your position clear in your own house. It is the mark of a hypocrite to be a Christian everywhere except at home.

Among your companions, do you acknowledge Christ as a friend whom you have found? In the shop and in the market, are you willing to be known as a man who has been washed in the blood of the Lamb? Do you long that all your dealings will be under the sweet rules of the gospel?

Reflection

How often do you "go public" and share the wonderful truths of Jesus?

To what degree do your deeds and words line up with what the Bible says—in your home, in your neighborhood, at work?

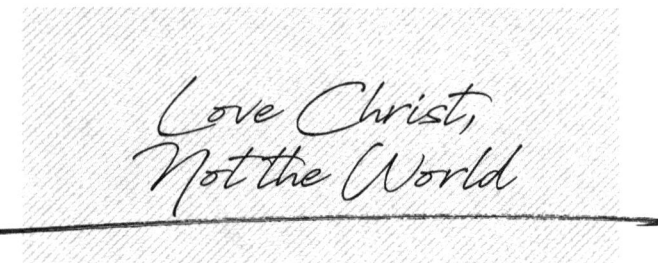

Love Christ, Not the World

"Walk in the Spirit, and you shall not fulfill
the lust of the flesh . . . And those who are
Christ's have crucified the flesh with its
passions and desires."

Galatians 5:16, 24

Has the world been crucified to you? Once it was your all—its praise, its riches, its songs and merrymaking. Has it been nailed to the cross in your sight? Oh, put your hand on your heart. Has it lost its burning desire after earthly things? Those who are Christs have crucified the flesh with its affections and lusts. Do you feel that Jesus has put the nails through your lusts? Do you wish they were dead?

You cannot glory in the cross and love the world. Ah, poor, deluded souls, you have never seen the glory of the way of pardon by Jesus. Go on, love the world. Grasp every pleasure. Gather heaps of money. Feed and fatten on your lusts. Take your fill. What will it profit you when you lose your soul?

Some people say, "Oh, that the world was crucified to me and I to the world! Oh, that my heart were as dead as a stone to the world and alive to Jesus!" Do you truly wish it? Look, then, to the cross. Behold the amazing gift of love. Sit down, like Mary, and gaze on a crucified Jesus. Then the world will become a dim, dying thing.

When you gaze at the sun, it makes everything else seem dark. When you taste honey, it makes everything else tasteless. Likewise, when your soul feeds on Jesus, it takes away the sweetness of all earthly things. Praise, pleasure, and fleshly lusts all lose their sweetness. Keep a continuous gaze. Run, looking toward Jesus. Look, until all the way of salvation by Jesus fills up the entire horizon, so glorious and peace speaking. Thus will the world be crucified to you, and you to the world.

Reflection

What happens when Christians try to "straddle the fence," courting the world and claiming to love Jesus?

Why is it impossible to "crucify the world" in our own strength?

Why do we have to focus on our relationship with Jesus in order to overcome our lusts?

Jesus: The Ultimate Source of Truth

"I am . . . the truth."

John 14:6

No doubt an unconverted man knows many truths. He may know the truths of mathematics and arithmetic; he may know many common, everyday truths. But still, it cannot be said that an unconverted man knows the truth because Christ is the truth.

Take away the keystone of an arch, and the whole arch becomes a heap of rubbish. The same stones may be there, but they are all fallen, smothered, and confused, without order, without end. Likewise, take Christ away, and the whole arch of truth becomes a heap of rubbish. The same truths may be there, but they are all fallen, without coherence, without order, without end.

Christ may be called the sun of the system of truth. Take the sun out of our solar system, and every planet would rush into confusion. The same planets would be there, but their conflicting forces would draw them hither and thither, orb dashing against orb in endless perplexity. Likewise, take Christ away, and the whole system of truth rushes into confusion. The same truths may be in the mind, but all conflicting and jarring in inextricable mazes because "the way of the wicked is like darkness; they do not know what makes them stumble" (Prov. 4:19). But let Christ be revealed to an unconverted soul, let it not be merely a man speaking about Christ to him, but let the Spirit of God reveal Him, and there is revealed, not a truth but *the truth.* You put the keystone into the arch of truth. You restore the sun to the center of the system. All truth becomes orderly and serviceable in that mind.

My friends, have you seen Christ, who is the truth? Then you know how true it is that in Him "are hidden all the treasures of wisdom and knowledge" (Col. 2:3), that He is "the Alpha and the Omega, the Beginning and the End" of all knowledge (Rev. 21:6).

Reflection

On what or whom do you base your view of truth? Why is the battle over the nature of truth becoming so divisive in our culture—even among Christians?

New Creation, New Desires

"God forbid that I should boast except in the
cross of our Lord Jesus Christ, by whom the
world has been crucified to me, and I to the
world."

Galatians 6:14

All who are truly Christ's are separated from
the world by the indwelling of the Holy Spirit.
"If anyone is in Christ, he is a new creation"
(2 Cor. 5:17). God gives him new desires. Once he desired
what other men do: praise of men, a name, power, money,
pleasures. These were the chief objects set before him.
Now these have lost their power over him. To him, the
world has become crucified. Now he desires more nearness
to God, more complete change of heart. He desires to
spread the knowledge of Jesus over the world.

Once all his sorrows were worldly sorrows; he wept
at the loss of friends or this world's possessions. But now
these sorrows are light afflictions. His heaviest grief now
is when the absence of the Spirit and burning of corruption within, or sin abounding around him, makes him
sigh and cry. That man is separated—he dwells in the
gardens.

Dear souls, have you been separated from the world?

Reflection

In what ways are you "separated" from the world?

What has God been revealing to you about your desires?

Ask Him to show you any desires, ambitions, or ways of thinking that hinder your spiritual growth and holy living.

God Hates Self-Righteousness

"For they being ignorant of God's righteousness, and seeking to establish their own righteousness, have not submitted to the righteousness of God."

Romans 10:3

Self-righteousness is the largest idol of the human heart, the idol that man loves most and God hates most. Dearly beloved, you will always be going back to this idol. You are always trying to be something in yourself, to gain God's favor by looking to your repentance, tears, and prayers, or by looking to your religious exercises. Beware of false christs. Study sanctification to the utmost, but don't make a christ of it. God hates self-righteousness more than all other gods because it comes in the place of Christ; it sits on Christ's throne. Dash self-righteousness down, dear friends. Let it never appear again.

Reflection

How does self-righteousness take the place of Christ?

What are some of the common ways by which people try to earn God's favor?

Get Rid of "Darling" Favorite Sins

"When I saw among the spoils a beautiful
Babylonian garment, two hundred shekels of
silver, and a wedge of gold weighing fifty
shekels, I coveted them and took them. And
there they are, hidden in the earth in the midst
of my tent, with the silver under it."

Joshua 7:21

E very man has his darling sins. Long they kept
you from the Lord Jesus. You have declared
that you were willing to leave them all for
Christ. Go home, then, and perform your vows. After
Hezekiah s passover, when they had enjoyed much of the
love and Spirit of God, "All Israel who were present went
out to the cities of Judah and broke the [pagan] sacred
pillars in pieces . . . and threw down the high places . . .
until they had utterly destroyed them all" (2 Chron. 31:1).
Go and do likewise. Do away with family idols, unholy
practices that have spread through your family. Do away
with secret idols in your own heart. Leave not one.
Remember, one Achan in the camp troubled Israel, and
they were smitten before their enemies (see Josh. 7:1-5).
So, one idol left in your heart may trouble you.

Reflection

Do you have any "darling" secret sins tucked away?

If so, what do you plan to do about them?

Think about the ways in which your unconfessed sins can block God's blessings.

The Source of True Life

"I am . . . the life."

John 14:6

Suppose it were possible for a dead limb to be joined into a living body so completely that all the veins would receive the purple tide of living blood. Suppose bone joins to bone, and sinew to sinew, and nerve to nerve. Would not that limb, however dead before, become a living limb? Before, it was cold, stiff, motionless, and full of corruption. Now it is warm, pliable, and full of life and motion. It is a living limb because it has joined to that which is life.

Or, suppose it's possible for a withered branch to be grafted into a living vine so completely that all the channels would receive the flow of generous sap. Do you not see that the branch, however dead before, becomes a living branch? Before, it was dry; fruitless, and withered. Now; it is full of sap, life, and vigor. It is a living branch because it is joined to the vine, which is its life. In the same w'ay, Christ is the life of every soul who cleaves to Him. He who is joined to the Lord is one spirit.

Is your soul like a dead limb—cold, stiff, motionless, and full of corruption? Cling to Christ. Be joined to Him by faith, and you will be one spirit. You will be made warm, vigorous, and full of activity in God's service. You will find it true that Christ is the life; your life will be bid with Christ in God. You wall say with the apostle, "It is no longer I who live, but Christ lives in me; and the life which I now live in the flesh I live by faith in the Son of God, who loved me and gave Himself for me" (Gal. 2:20).

Reflection

Is Christ truly your source of life?

Why do other sources lead away from life?

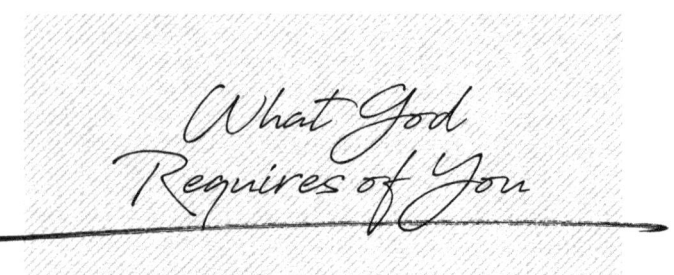
What God Requires of You

"What does the Lord require of you but to
do justly, to love mercy, and to walk humbly
with your God?"

Micah 6:8

W hat does the Lord require of you? Consider these three commands that the prophet Micah specified:

God requires His redeemed ones to be holy. If you are His brethren. He will have you be righteous and holy. He requires that you do justly; be just in your dealings with other people. This is one of His own glorious features. He is a just God. "He is my rock, and there is no unrighteousness in Him" (Ps. 92:15). Have you come to Him through Jesus? He requires you to reflect His image. Are you His child? You must be like Him. Brethren, be exact in your dealings. Be like your God. Take care of dishonesty and trickery in business. Take care when raising the prices of your goods when selling them and lowering them down when buying them. "'It is good for nothing,' cries the buyer; but when he has gone his way, then he boasts" (Prov. 20:14). It shall not be so among you. God requires you do to justly.

He requires you to love mercy. This is the brightest feature in the character of Christ. If you are in Christ, drink deeply of His Spirit. God requires you to be merciful. The world is selfish, unmerciful. Be merciful, as your Father in heaven is merciful.

He requires you to walk humbly with your God. Christ says, "Learn from Me, for I am gentle and lowly in heart" (Matt. 11:29). If God has covered all your black sins, rebellions, and failings, then never open your mouth except in humble praise.

God requires this at your hand. Walk with God, and walk humbly.

Reflection

Compare the way you live life with the points in this reading. How can you apply those three requirements—justice, mercy, and humility—to your daily life?

Draw Strength from Christ's Grace

"For with You is the fountain of life."

Psalm 36:9

Whatever Christ requires. He gives us grace to perform. Christ is not only good as our way to the Father, but He is our fountain of living waters. Be strong in the grace that is in Christ Jesus. There is enough in Christ to supply the needs of all His people. There are unsearchable riches in Him.

Be strong in the grace that is in Him. Live out of yourself, and live upon Him. Go and tell Him, since He requires all this of you, that He must give you grace according to your need. "My God shall supply all your need according to His riches in glory by Christ Jesus" (Phil. 4:19). Now lean upon Him, get life from Him that will never die, get living water from Him that will never dry up. Let His hand hold you up amidst the billows of this tempestuous sea. Let His shoulder carry you over the thorns of this wilderness.

Reflection

How can you tap
more deeply into the
riches of Christ as
needs arise?

In practical terms,
what's involved in
"leaning on" Him?

Every Christian Faces Spiritual Warfare

"I see another law in my members, warring
against the law of my mind, and bringing me
into captivity to the law of sin which is in my
members."

Romans 7:23

There never can be absolute peace in the bosom
of a believer, so long as we dwell on earth.
There certainly is peace with God, but constant war with sin. This law in the members has an army
of lusts under him, and he wages war against the law of
God. Sometimes, indeed, an army is lying in ambush,
and the enemies lie quiet until a favorable moment comes.
Likewise, in the heart, lusts often lie quiet until the hour
of temptation, and they war against the soul. The heart
is like a volcano. Sometimes it slumbers and sends up
nothing but a little smoke, but the fire is slumbering all
the while below and will soon break out again.

There are two great combatants in the believers soul.
There is Satan on the one side, with the flesh and all its
lusts at his command. Then, on the other side, there is
the Holy Spirit, with the new creature at His command.
And so "the flesh lusts against the Spirit, and the Spirit
against the flesh; and these are contrary to one another,
so that you do not do the things that you wish" (Gal. 5:17).

Is Satan ever successful? In the deep wisdom of God,
the law in the members sometimes brings the soul into

captivity. Noah was a perfect man who walked with God, and yet he was led captive. "[Noah] drank of the wine and was drunk" (Gen. 9:21). Abraham was the friend of God (see Isa. 41:8), yet he told a lie, saying of Sarah his wife, "She is my sister" (Gen. 20:2). Job, a perfect man who feared God and hated evil, was provoked to curse the day he was horn (see Job 3:1). We could give similar examples of Moses, David, Solomon, Hezekiah, Peter, and the apostles.

Have you experienced this warfare? It is a clear mark of God's children. We must ever strive for God's perfection, but accept His grace when we inevitably fall short.

Reflection

In which "weak spots" does Satan attack you?
Why is it important to recognize that a spiritual battle is being fought within you?

Jesus, Our Intercessor, Gives Us Joy

"These things I have spoken to you, that My
joy may remain in you, and that your joy may
be full."

John 15:11

W hen Christ ascended from the Mount of
Olives and passed through the heavens,
carrying His bloody wounds into God's
presence, and when His disciples had gazed after Him
until a cloud received Him out of their sight, they returned to Jerusalem with great joy (see Luke 24:52).
Were they joyful at parting with the blessed Master?
When He told them He would leave them, sorrow had
filled their hearts, and He had to argue with them and
comfort them, saying, "Let not your heart be troubled .
. . I go to prepare a place for you" (John 14:1-2). How,
then, were they changed? Jesus has left them, and they
are filled with joy. Here is the secret: They knew Christ
was going into God's presence for them, that their great
High Priest was entering within the veil to make intercession for them.

Believer, would you share in the disciples' great joy?
Consider the place of Jesus, who is the High Priest and
Intercessor. He is above the clouds and sky so that you
would stand gazing up into heaven, not with the bodily
eye but with the eye of faith. How wonderful the eye of

faith is. It sees beyond the stars, pierces to God's throne, and there looks on the face of Jesus making intercession for us, whom having not seen we love; in whom, though now we see Him not, yet believing, we rejoice with joy unspeakable and full of glory (see 1 Peter 1:8).

If you would live thus, what sweet peace would fill you! And how many blessings of the Spirit would come down on you in answer to the Savior's prayer. How your face would shine like Stephens, and the poor blind world would see that there is a joy the world cannot give and cannot take away, a heaven on earth.

Reflection

Why does Jesus intercede for us in heaven?
If Jesus were talking with you today, what might He say about your level of joy?

Care for the Needy

"He who has mercy on the poor, happy is he."
Proverbs 14:21

Christ's poor are our brothers and sisters. Do you do what you can for them? In the great day, Christ will say to those on His right hand, "Come, you blessed of My Father . . . for I was hungry and you gave Me food" (Matt. 25:34—35). They stand in the place of Christ. Christ no longer stands in need of Mary's ointment, Marthas hospitality, or the Samaritans drink of water. He is beyond the reach of these things and will never need them again. But He has left many of His brothers and sisters behind in this world—some diseased, some lame, some like Lazarus all covered with sores. And He says, "Inasmuch as you did it to one of the least of these My brethren, you did it to Me" (Matt. 25:40).

Do you live simply so that you will have more to give away? Do you not buy more clothes—perhaps unnecessary anyway—so that you may be able to clothe the naked? Are you willing to eat less, or less indulgently, so the impoverished may eat at all? Jesus' admonition to care for the needy was not merely a *suggestion*, but a *commandment*.

Reflection

In what ways do you care for those less fortunate?

How might simplifying your lifestyle enable you to do more for people in Jesus' name?

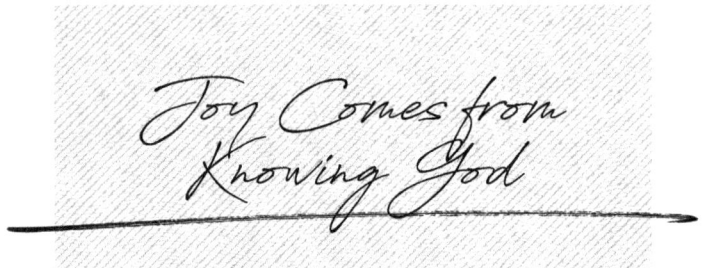

Joy Comes from Knowing God

"The fruit of the Spirit is love, joy."

Galatians 5:22

No joy is like the divine joy. It is infinite, full, eternal, pure, unmingled joy. It is light, without any cloud to darken it. It is calm, without any breath to ruffle it. Clouds and darkness are round about Jesus, storms and fire go before Him, but within all is peace inexpressible and unchangeable.

Believers in some measure share in this joy. You can look on all events with a calm, holy joy, knowing that your Fathers will and purposes alone will stand.

Reflection

Is joy a prominent
characteristic of
your life?
If not, why not?
Thank God for His
faithfulness, for
working out His
will and purposes in
your life.

Springs of Living Water

"He who believes in Me, as the Scripture has said, out of his heart will flow rivers of living water."

John 7:38

If you have believed in Jesus, you have received the Spirit, and from you there must be flowing rivers of living water. Is this the case? Alas, how many of you must answer, "No, we don't know what you mean."

Are there not some whose heart is more like a sinkhole of despair than a fountain of living water? Are there not some who send forth from their heart rivers that pollute and poison every place they go? Are there not some who send forth streams of horrid imaginations and impure desires? Are there not some who are like a fountain sealed? They seem to come to Jesus, but they do not give out any living stream. This is cause for great concern.

Every person who believes in the Lord Jesus must receive the Spirit. Every person who receives the Spirit will make Him manifest by sending forth rivers of living water. Be not deceived, my dear friends. He who does righteousness is righteous. If you are living a dead, useless life, you are no Christian.

Reflection

Is your life a spring
of living water?

Prayerfully examine
your life, asking
God to reveal to you
any areas in which
you are polluting
rather than
providing living
water.

Know Jesus, Know Peace

"My peace I give to you, not as the world
gives do I give to you."

John 14:27

L earn the true way of coming to peace—by looking to Jesus. Some of you think you will come to peace by looking into your own heart. Your eyes are riveted there. You watch every change there. If you could only see the glimpse of light there, oh, what joy it would give you! If you could only see a melting of your stony heart. If you could only see your heart turning to God. If you could only see a glimpse of the image of Jesus in your heart, you would be at peace. But you cannot. All is dark within.

Dear soul, it is not there that you will find peace. You must avert the eye from your heart altogether. You must look to a declared Christ. Spread out the record of God concerning His Son. The Gospels are the narrative of the heart of Jesus, of the work of Jesus, of the grace of Jesus. Spread them out before the eye of your mind until they fill your eye. Cry for the Spirit to breathe over the page— to make a manifested Christ stand out plainly before you. The moment you are willing to believe all that is spoken there concerning Jesus, that moment you will wipe away your tears, and exchange your sighs for a new song of praise.

Reflection

What is your
definition of peace?
Why is it important
to look to Jesus
rather than looking
elsewhere for peace?

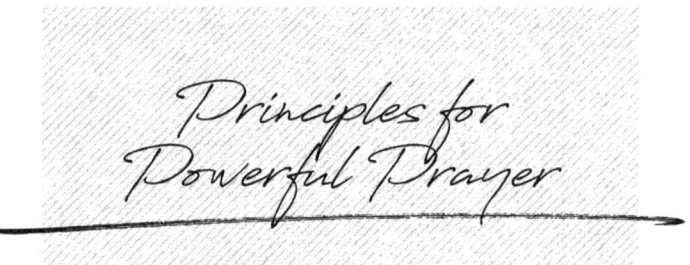

Principles for Powerful Prayer

"For through Him we both have access by
one Spirit to the Father."

Ephesians 2:18

When a believer prays, he is not alone. There are three with him: the Father seeing in secret, His ear open; the Son blotting out sin and offering up the prayer; the Holy Spirit quickening and giving desires. There can be no true prayer without these three.

Some pray without the Father. They do not feel. They are speaking to the back of their chair, to the world, or to the air.

Some pray without the Son. They come in their own name, in their own righteousness. That is the sacrifice of fools.

Some pray without the Holy Spirit. These are not filled with divine breathings.

Dear friends, if you would live, you must pray, and if you would pray with acceptance, you must pray to the Father in the name of Jesus and by His Spirits quickening. Pray without ceasing. Whatever you need, ask God immediately. Have set times of approaching God solemnly. Let nothing interfere with these times.

Reflection

Are you satisfied
with your prayer
life?
What choices might
you make in order
to establish a more
disciplined and
richer prayer life?

We Are Just Passing Through

"Do not love the world or the things in the
world If anyone loves the world, the love of
the Father is not in him."

1 John 2:15

To a child of God, this world is a wilderness. Everything is fading here; nothing is abiding. Money takes wings and flees away. Friends die. All are like grass, and if some are more beautiful or engaging than others, still they are only like the flower of the grass—a little more ornamented, but often withering sooner. Sometimes a worldly comfort is like Jonah's plant; it came up over his head to be a shadow to deliver him from his grief (see Jonah 4:6-8). So Jonah was exceedingly thankful for the plant. But God prepared a worm, and when the morning rose the next day, the worm attacked the plant so it withered. Likewise, our worldly comfort sometimes grows up over our head like a shadow, and we are exceedingly glad for our gourd. But God prepares a worm; we faint and are ready to die.

Here we have no continuing city, but we seek one to come. This is a wilderness: Arise, depart, this is not your rest because it is polluted. An experienced Christian views everything here as temporary. Things that are seen are temporal; things that are unseen are eternal.

Everything is stained with sin here, even the natural

scenery of this world. The thorns and thistles tell of a cursed earth. "We are of God, and the whole world lies under the sway of the wicked one" (1 John 5:19). If we had no body of sin, what a sweet glory would appear in everything. We would sing like the birds in the spring.

Reflection

Which particular things of the world tempt you the most? How can you focus more effectively on the eternal life to come and on the holy person God calls you to be?

Receive the Joy of God's Presence

"Be glad in the Lord and rejoice, you righteous; and shout for joy, all you upright in heart!"

Psalm 32:11

Creature joys only fill a small part of the soul. Money, houses, land, music, entertainment, friends—these all provide joy, but they are just *drops* of joys. Christ revealed makes the cup run over. As the palmist said, "You anoint my head with oil: my cup runs over" (23:5). Believing in a manifested Christ fills the heart full of joy. "In Your presence is fullness of joy" (Ps. 16:11). Christ brings the soul into God's presence. One smile of God fills the heart more than ten thousand smiles of the world.

You who have nothing but creature joy, hunting after butterflies, feeding on carrion, why do you spend money for that which is not bread? You who are afflicted, tempest-tossed, and not comforted, look to a manifested Jesus. "According to your faith let it be to you" (Matt. 9:29). Believe nothing, and you will have no joy. Believe little, and you will have little joy. Believe much, and you will have much joy. Believe all, and you will have all joy.

Reflection

Where do you find
your joy?
What is the
relationship
between your faith
and the joy you
receive from God?

Christ, Our Example

"Which of you convicts Me of sin?"

John 8:46

C hrist not only became man, but it behooved Him to be made like us in all things. He was different from us in only two ways, in being God as well as man and in being without sin. In the manger at Bethlehem lay a perfect infant, but also Jehovah. That mysterious person, who rode on an ass's colt and wept over Jerusalem, was as much a man as you are, and as much God as the Father is. The tears He shed were human tears, yet the Jehovah's love swelled below His mantle. That pale person who hung quivering on the cross was indeed man; human blood flowed from His wounds, but He was as truly God.

Christ was the only one in human form of whom it can be said that He was holy, harmless, undefiled, and separate from sinners. He was the only One on whom God could look down from heaven and say, "This is My beloved Son, in whom I am well pleased" (Matt. 3:17). We have used every member of our body and faculty of our mind as servants of sin. Every member of His body and faculty of His mind were used only as servants to holiness. His mouth was the only human mouth from which none but gracious words proceeded. His eye was the only human eye that never shot forth flames of pride, envy, or lust. His hand was the only human hand that never stretched forth to do anything but good. His heart was the only human heart that wasn't deceitful above all tilings and desperately wicked.

Reflection

What does this reading reveal about Christ and the type of life He calls each of us to live? Why can we know for sure that He understands what we face every day?

Freedom from Sinful Habits

"How shall we who died to sin live any longer in it? . . . If we have been united together in the likeness of His death, certainly we also shall be in the likeness of His resurrection."

Romans 6:2, 5

I s there one of you desirous of being made new, of being delivered from the slavery of sinful habits and affections? We can point you to no other remedy but the love of Christ. Behold how He loved you! See what He bore for you. Put your finger, as it were, into the prints of the nails and thrust your hand into His side. Be faithless no more, but believing.

Under a sense of your sin, flee to the Savior of sinners. As the timorous dove flies to hide itself in the crevices of the rock, so flee to hide yourself in the wounds of your Savior. And when you have found Him, like the shadow of a great rock in a weary land, when you sit under His shadow with great delight, you wall find that He has slain all the hostility, that He has accomplished all your warfare.

God is now for you. Planted together with Christ in the likeness of His death, you will be also in the likeness of His resurrection. Dead to sin, you will be alive to God.

Reflection

What does it mean
to be "dead to sin"?

What sins do you
need help
overcoming?

Ask God to make
His healing,
powerful presence
known to you.

The Suffering of Christ

"Paul, as his custom was, went in to them,
and for three Sabbaths reasoned with them
from the Scriptures, explaining and
demonstrating that the Christ had to suffer
and rise again from the dead."

Acts 17:2-3

Jesus tasted the difficulties of many situations. The first thirty years. He tasted the trials of working for His daily bread. Then He subsisted on the kindness of others. Certain women who followed Him gave to Him of their substance. He had no place to lay His head, spending many nights on the Mount of Olives or on the hills of Galilee. He bore the trials of a gospel minister. He preached from morning until night. How often He was grieved In people's unbelief; He marveled at their unbelief: "O faithless and perverse generation, how long shall I be with you? How long shall I bear with you?" (Matt. 17:17). How often He offended many by His preaching! How often they hated Him for His love!

What trials He had from His own family! Even His own brothers didn't believe in Him but mocked. The people of His town tried to throw Him over the rocks. What trials He had from Satan! Believers complain about Satan, but they never felt his power as Christ did. What an awful conflict took place during forts class in the wilderness! How fearfully Satan urged on Pharisees,

Herod, and Judas to torment Christ. What trials He had from God! Believers often groan under the hidings of God's countenance, but they seldom taste even a drop of what Christ drank. What dreadful agony He experienced in Gethsemane.

Throughout eternity, we will study these sufferings. Learn the amazing love of Christ, that He left glory for such a condition. Learn to bear sufferings cheerfully. You have not yet suffered as Christ did.

Reflection

Ponder the suffering Jesus experienced for you. Ask Him to give you the strength to endure difficult situations and to keep trusting Him—the one who loves you more than you can ever comprehend.

Because God Loves Us, He Disciplines Us

"My son, do not despise the chastening of the Lord,
nor be discouraged when you are rebuked by Him;
for whom the Lord loves He chastens, and scourges
every son whom He receives . . . No chastening seems
to be joyful for the present, but painful, nevertheless,
afterward it yields the peaceable fruit of
righteousness to those who have been trained by it."

Hebrews 12:5-6, 11

I t is a sad thing when the soul faints under God's rebukes. They were intended to lead you deeper into Christ, into a fuller enjoyment of God. Do not faint when He rebukes you. When a soul comes to Christ, he expects to be led to heaven on a green, soft pathway, without a thorn or thistle. On the contrary, he is led into darkness, poverty stares him in the face, bereavement leaves him desolate, or persecutions embitter his life. Now his soul remembers the wormwood and gall. He forgets the love and wisdom that are dealing with him and says, "I am the man who has seen affliction. The Lord has forsaken me; my God has forgotten me."

The way of God is not always easy or comfortable. But the ultimate triumph will render all earthly hardship but a vapor, erased from memory by eternal delights.

Reflection

How do you
respond when God
disciplines you?

Why does God
discipline those He
loves?

Guard Your Conscience

"I myself always strive to have a conscience
without offense toward God and men."

Acts 24:16

As long as a believer walks humbly with his God, his soul is at peace. The candle of the Lord shines on his head. He walks in the light as God is in the light, and the blood of Jesus Christ His Son cleanses him from all sin. But the moment unbelief creeps in, he is led away into sin; like David, he falls very low. A believer generally falls lower than the world, and now he falls into darkness.

When Adam fell, he was afraid. He hid himself from God among the trees of the garden and made a covering of leaves. Alas! When a believer falls, he also is afraid; he hides from God. Now he has lost a good conscience; he fears to meet with God. He does not love the house of prayer; his heart is now filled with suspicions. This is the most bitter of all kinds of desertion. If you put away faith and a good conscience, you will suffer shipwreck.

Reflection

Ask God to reveal
to you anything
sinful that is a
barrier between you
and Him.

Then confess your
sinfulness and get
your conscience
clear again.

God's Amazing Love

"Behold what manner of love the Father has
bestowed on us, that we should be called
children of God!"

1 John 3:1

A mother's love is the fullest love that we have on earth. She loses with all her heart. But there is no love as full as that of God toward His Son. God loves Jesus fully. The whole heart of the Father is, as it were, continually poured down in love on the Lord Jesus. There is nothing in Christ except what draws the infinite love of God. In Him, God sees His own image perfect, His own law acted out, His own will done. The Father loves the Son fully; but when a soul comes into Christ, the same love rests on that soul: "that the love with which You loved Me may be in them" (John 17:26).

True, a creature cannot receive God's love as Jesus can, but it is the same love that shines on us and Him— full, satisfying, unbounded lose. When the sun pours down its beams on the wide ocean and on a little floss'er at the same time, the same sunshine is poured into both, although the ocean has a vastly larger capacity to receive its glorious beams. So it is the same love that pours down on the Savior and the sinner, although Jesus is able to contain more.

How can God forget what He fully loves? If God fully loves you. He has not forgotten you; He can't forget you. A creature's love may fail, because what is a creature? A clay vessel, a breath of wind that passes away and doesn't return. But the Creators love can't fail; it is full of love toward an object infinitely worthy of His love, in which you share.

Reflection

What does it mean to you that God accepts you *just as you are*? Praise Him for His love, and draw closer to Jesus.

When Tempted, Stand Firm

"For in that He Himself has suffered, being tempted, He is able to aid those who are tempted."

Hebrews 2:18

All believers are a tempted people. Even day they have trials; even time is to them a time of need. The unconverted are little tempted. They don't feel temptations rising in their hearts, nor do they know Satan's power. Before conversion, a man believes as little in the Devil as he believes in Christ. But when a man comes to Christ, he becomes a tempted soul.

God at times brings His child into a situation where faith will be tried. Sometimes He exalts him to see if he wall turn proud and forget Him. Sometimes He brings him low to see if he will murmur against God. Blessed in the man who endures temptations. Sometimes God brings people into a strait, where the trial is, to see whether they will believe in Him alone or trust in flesh and blood.

The world tempts a child of God. It watches for missteps. It loves nothing more than to see a child of God fall into sin; it soothes the world's conscience to think that all are equally bad.

The heart of God's children is a fountain of temptation.

Sometimes it says, "What harm is there in that? It is a little sin," or "I will just sin this once and never again," or "I will repent afterward and be saved."

Satan hurls his fiery darts. He terrifies God's children away from Christ, disturbs them during prayer, fills their mind with blasphemies, and hounds the world against them.

Believers, you are a tempted people. You are always poor and needy. And God intends it should be so, to give you constant reasons to go to Jesus.

Reflection

How do you respond when temptations come? How committed are you to resisting them through the power of Christ?

Jesus Christ: Our High Priest

"Therefore He is also able to save to the
uttermost those who come to God through
Him, since He always lives to make
intercession for them."

Hebrews 7:25

We have a merciful and faithful High Priest. He endured temptation so that He might aid those who are tempted. The high priest of old did not only offer sacrifice at the altar; his work was not done when the lamb was consumed. He was to be a father to Israel. He went in and prayed for them within the veil. He came out and blessed the people, saying, "The Lord bless you and keep you; the Lord make His face shine upon you, and be gracious to you" (Num. 6:24-25).

So it is with the Lord Jesus. His work was not all done on Calvary. He who died for our sins lives to pray for us, to help during every time of need. He is still man on the right hand of God. He is still God, and therefore, by reason of His divinity, is present here this day as much as any of us. He knows your every sorrow, trial, and difficulty. He hears every half-breathed sigh and brings in notice thereof to His human heart at the right hand of God. His human heart is the same yesterday, today, and forever. It pleads for you, thinks about you, and plans deliverance for you.

Reflection

Why do we need a
heavenly High
Priest?

In what ways does
He help us?

Shine for God

"Become blameless and harmless, children of God without fault in the midst of a crooked and perverse generation, among whom you shine as lights in the world."

Philippians 2:15

Make it the business of your life to shine. If the sun were to grow weary of running its daily journey and were to quit shining, would you not say that it should be taken down? Didn't God hang it in the sky to give light to the earth? Just so, dear Christians, if you grow weary in well-doing, in shining with Christ's beauty, in walking by Christ's Spirit, you also should he taken down and east away. Did not Christ arise upon you for this very end, that you might be a light in the world? Ah, think of this, dark and useless Christians who are putting your candles under a bushel. I tremble for some w'ho will not lay themselves out for Christ. Ah, you are wronging yourselves and dishonoring Christ. Your truest happiness is in shining. The more you shine for Christ, the happier you will be. "For to me, to live is Christ, and to die is gain" (Phil. 1:21).

Learn a lesson from the sun. It shines both far and near; it does not pour its beams all into one sunny valley or onto one bright land. No, it journeys on from shore to shore, pouring its rich beams on the wide ocean,

Africa's torrid sands, and Greenland's icy coasts. Go and do likewise. Shine as lights in the world.

Shine in your closet in secret prayer. Let your face shine in secret communion with God. Shine in your family in your town, so that when you mingle with the crowd, it may be as if an angel shook his wings. Shine in the world; embrace every shore with the beams of living love.

Reflection

Do you agree that the more a person shines for Christ, the happier he or she will be?

How can you obtain more of Christs "light" so that you can radiate Jesus' love and guide people to Him?

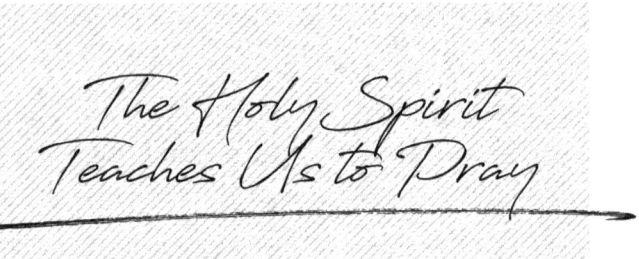

The Holy Spirit Teaches Us to Pray

"Praying always with all prayer and
supplication in the Spirit."

Ephesians 6:18

The Holy Spirit drove an ungodly Manasseh to his knees. Manasseh had often bowed the knee in youth at his godly father's knee; he had often prayed to his bloody idols; he had often prayed to the Devil. But now, when the Spirit came, he began to pray indeed (see 2 Chron. 33:12).

The Holy Spirit drove a blaspheming Paul to his knees. Often Paul had prayed at the feet of Gamaliel. In the synagogue and at the corners of streets, he had made long prayers for pretense. Now, awakened by the Spirit of God, "Behold, he is praying" (Acts 9:11).

Have you been taught to pray by the Spirit of God? You once had a form, or you prayed for a pretense, but have you been driven to pray by the Holy Spirit? Then you may be sure He has begun a work in your heart.

A prayerless soul is an unawakened soul—very near to being burned. Some pieces of wood will bum much more easily than others. Some pieces are green and don't readily catch fire, but a dry piece of wood is easily kindled. Prayerless souls are dry pieces of wood.

Reflection

Are you drawn to pray, to know God better?

What challenges do you face in building a stronger prayer life?

What are some practical steps you will take to overcome these challenges?

Keep the Door to Your Heart Open

"Behold, I stand at the door and block. If anyone hears My voice and opens the door, I will come in to him and dine with him, and he with Me."

Revelation 3:20

C hrist is the Shepherd who seeks the lost sheep, but it is as true that He is seeking His own people also, that He may make His abode with them, that their joy may be full. Christ is not done with a soul when He has brought it to the forgiveness of sins. Only then He begins His regular visits to the soul.

In the daily reading of the Word, Christ pays daily visits to sanctify the believing soul. In daily prayer, Christ reveals Himself to His own, in other ways than He does to the world. In the house of God, Christ comes in to His own and says, "Peace be unto you!" In the sacrament, He makes Himself known to them in the breaking of bread, and they cry out, "It is the Lord!" These are all appointed times when the Savior comes to visit His own.

Even believers have doors on their hearts. You'd think, perhaps, that when once Christ had found an entrance into a poor sinners heart, He never would find difficulty in getting in anymore. You'd think that as Samson carried off the gates of Gaza, bar and all, so Christ would earn, away all the gates and bars from believing hearts. But no, there is still a door on the heart, and Christ stands and knocks. He desires to he inside. It is not His pleasure that we should sit lonely and desolate. He desires to come in to us, dine with us, and we with Him.

Reflection

If Jesus were sitting across from you right now, what would He say about the condition of your heart?
How often do you open your heart to Him?

When Troubles Come, Lean on Christ

"God has not given us a spirit of fear, but of power and of love and of a sound mind."

2 Timothy 1:7

When worldly comforts abound, then the consolations of Christ do little abound. It is not when the world is full of smiles and kindness that a true believer has the sweetest visits of the Savior. It is rather when the believer is left like an orphan, when comforts are withdrawn, when friends die or prove to be untrue, when the bleak world appears to be chilling, then Jesus comes in and says, "Peace to you." The brightest gleams of sunshine are those that come through the darkest clouds. Likewise, the sweetest visits of the Savior occur when the doors of worldly comfort are shut.

Are you a believer? You will have troubles, but you will have Christ with them all.

Reflection

To whom or what do you turn when difficulties slam against you?

Do you agree that Christs sweetest visits occur during your most difficult times?

Why or why not?

feeling far from God?

"Blessed be the God and Father of our Lord
Jesus Christ, who according to His abundant
mercy has begotten us again to a living hope
through the resurrection of Jesus Christ
from the dead."

1 Peter 1:3

Are you a believer in darkness anxiously seeking Christ? You thought that you had really been a believer in Jesus, but you have fallen into sin and darkness, and all your evidences are overclouded. You are anxiously seeking Christ. Your soul yearns for His word. You seek and call, even though you get no answer. You search the Bible, even though it brings no comfort to you. You pray, though you have no comfort in prayer, no confidence that you are heard. You ask for counsel from His ministers and, when they deal plainly with you, you are not offended. They wound you and take away the veil from you. They tell you not to rely on any past experiences that may have been delusive and only increase anxiety. Still you follow after Christ. You seek the people of Christ and tell them to pray for you.

Is this your situation? Do you see your own image here? Do you feel that you cannot rest out of Christ? If so, do not be too cast down. This is no mark that you are not a believer, but the very opposite. Say, "Why are you cast down, O my soul? And why are you disquieted within me? Hope in God, for I shall yet praise Him for the help of His countenance" (Ps. 42:5).

Reflection

When you feel far away from God, what is usually the cause?

Why is it important not to depend on how we feel during those times, but on what we know to be true of God and His Word?

Confronting Pride

"A thorn in the flesh was given to me, a
messenger of Satan to buffet me, lest I be
exalted above measure."

2 Corinthians 12:7

Whatever the thorn was that made Paul groan,
one thing is plain: It was a truly humbling
experience. It brought Paul to the dust. Why
was this given to him? To keep him from being exalted
above measure. This is stated twice (see 2 Cor. 12:7).

What a singular thing is pride! A natural man is
proud of anything. Proud of his person, although he did
not make it, yet he prides himself on his looks. Proud of
his dress, although a block of wood might have the same
cause for pride if you would put clothes on it. Proud of
riches, as if there were some merit in having more gold
than others. Proud of status, as if there were some merit
in having noble blood.

Pride flow's through the veins, yet there is a pride
more wonderful than that of nature—pride of grace. You
would think a man never could be proud who had once
seen himself lost, yet Scripture shows a man may be
proud of his measure of grace, proud of forgiveness, proud
of humility, and proud of knowing more about God than
other people. This pride was springing up in Paul's heart
when God sent him the thorn in the flesh.

Reflection

Where does pride
show up in your
life?

What are some
reasons why pride is
so dangerous?

We Are Always in God's Hands

"Now to Him who is able to keep you from
stumbling, and to present you faultless before
the presence of His glory with exceeding
joy."

Jude v. 24

L earn, dear brothers and sisters, the true glory
of a Christian in this world. The world knows
nothing about it. A true Christian has a body
of sin. He has every lust and corruption that is in the
heart of man or devil. He wants no tendency to sin. If
the Lord has given you light, you know and feel this.

What is the difference, then, between you and the
world? Infinite! You are in the hand of Christ. His Spirit
is within you. He is able to keep you from stumbling. "Be
glad in the Lord and rejoice, you righteous; and shout
for joy, all you upright in heart" (Ps. 32:11)!

Reflection

How does being "in God's hands" apply to your daily life?

Thank God today for His grace and mercy toward you, for standing with you during difficult times and enabling you to stand firm against sin.

A Firm Foundation

"No other foundation can anyone lay than
that which is laid, which is Jesus Christ."

1 Corinthians 3:11

Just as every stone of a building rests on the foundation, so does every believer rest on Christ. He is the foundation rock on which all believers rest. If it were not for the foundation, the whole house would fall into ruins; the floods and wands would sweep it away. If it w'ere not for Christ, all believers would be swept away by God's anger, but they are rooted and built up in him, so they form His house.

The hands of Christ have placed every stone of the building. He has taken every stone from the quarry. Look toward the rock from which you were hewed and the hole of the pit from which you were dug. A natural person is embedded in the world just as firmly as rock in the quarry; the hands of the almighty Savior alone can dig out the soul and loosen it from its natural state.

See to it that you are quarried out by Christ. See to it that you are carried by Him and built on Him. Then you wall be a habitation of God through the Holy Spirit.

Reflection

Are you building
your life on the
foundation of
Christ?

In contrast, what
kind of foundations
does our culture
promote?

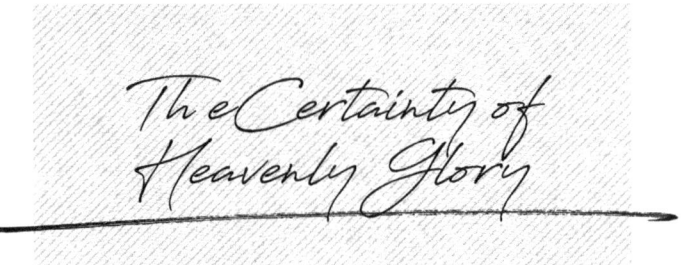

The Certainty of Heavenly Glory

"In My Father's house are many mansions; if it were not so, I would have told you. I go to prepare a place for you."

John 14:2

When a family is going to emigrate to a foreign country, often the oldest brother goes beforehand to prepare a place for his younger siblings. This is what Christ has done. He doesn't intend for us to live here always; He has gone on a far journey in order to prepare a place for us.

Oh Christians, believe in Christ preparing a place for you. It will greatly take away the fear of dying. It is an awful thing to die, even for a forgiven and sanctified soul, to enter a world unknown, unseen, and untried. One thing takes away fear; Christ is preparing a place quite suitable for my soul. He knows all the wants and weaknesses of my frame. I know He will make it a pleasant home for me.

Reflection

What do you think
of when you think
of heaven?

How important do
you think it is to
remember heaven
during your
everyday activities?

Be Active and Useful

"Be doers of the word, and not hearers only,
deceiving yourselves."

James 1:22

I t is very striking to see the uselessness of many Christians. Are there none of you who know what it is to be selfish in your Christianity? You have seen a selfish child go into a secret place to enjoy some delicious morsels undisturbed by his companions. So it is with some Christians. They feed on Christ and forgiveness, but it is alone and all for themselves.

Aren't there some of you who can enjoy being a Christian while your dearest friend is not, and yet you will not speak to him? See here, you have your work to do. When Christ found you. He said, "Go, work in My vineyard!" What were you hired for, if it was not to work? What were you saved for, if it was not to spread salvation? What were you blessed for?

My Christian friends, how little you live as if you were servants of Christ. How much idle time and idle talk you have. This is not like a good servant. How many things you have to do for yourself! How few for Christ and His people. This is not like a servant.

Reflection

Which person(s) came to mind as you read this?

What is involved in being a servant of Christ?

What work has He specifically called you to do for Him and His kingdom?

Focus on Christ, Not Yourself

"Let us lay aside every weight, and the sin which so easily ensnares us, and let us rim with endurance the race that is set before us, looking unto Jesus, the author and finisher of our faith, who for the joy that was set before Him endured the cross, despising the shame, and has sat down at the right hand of the throne of God."

Hebrews 12:1-2

Jesus is on the throne of heaven. Consider Him. Look long and earnestly on His wounds, on His glory. Do you think it would he safe to trust Him? Do you think His sufferings and obedience will have been enough?

Let me ever stand and gaze on the almighty, all-worthy, all divine Savior until my soul drinks in complete assurance that His work undertaken for sinners is a finished work. Yes, though the sins of all the world were on my wicked head, still I could not doubt that His work is complete and that I am quite safe when I believe in Him.

Some of you have really been brought by God to believe in Jesus. Yet you have no abiding peace and very little growing in holiness. Why is this? It is because your eye is fixed anywhere but on Christ. You are so busy looking at books, looking at men, or looking at the world that you have no time, no heart for looking at Christ.

No wonder you have little peace and joy in believing. No wonder you live such an inconsistent and unholy life.

Change your plan. Consider the greatness and glory of Christ, who has undertaken all on the behalf of sinners, and you would find it quite impossible to walk in darkness or in sin. Lift your eyes from your own bosom, downcast believer. Look on Jesus. It is good to consider your ways, but it is far better to consider Christ.

Reflection

What has Jesus accomplished in your life? What types of things distract you from being focused on Him—and the peace He longs to give you, the holiness He desires to cultivate in you?

Allow Christ to Love You

"We love Him because He first loved us."

1 John 4:19

W hen a poor sinner clings to Jesus and finds the forgiving love of God, lie cannot but love God back again. When the prodigal returned home and felt his father's arms around his neck, then did he feel the gushings of affection toward his father. When the summer sun shines down fully on the sea, it draws the vapors upward to the sky. Likewise, when the sunbeams of the Son of Righteousness fall on the soul, they draw forth the constant risings of love to him in return.

Some of you are longing to be able to love God. Come into His love then. Consent to be loved by Him, though worthless in yourself. It is better to be loved by Him than to love, and it is the only way to learn to love Him. When the light of the sun falls on the moon, it finds the moon dark and unlovely, but the moon reflects the light and casts it back again. So let the love of God shine into your heart, and you will cast it back again. The only cure for a cold heart is to look at the heart of Jesus.

Reflection

Do you feel loved by God?

Why or why not?

Why is it sometimes hard to feel Gods love?

Love Other Believers

"Walk in love, as Christ also has loved us and given Himself for us."

Ephesians 5:2

I f you love an absent person, you will love his or her photograph. What does the sailor's wife keep so closely wrapped in her nightstand among sweet-smelling flowers and precious things? She takes it out morning and evening, and gazes at it through her tears. It is the photograph of her absent husband. She loves it because it is like him. It has many imperfections, but still it is like him.

Believers are the photographs of God in this world. The Spirit of Christ dwells in them. They walk as He walked. True, they are full of imperfections, yet they are true copies. If you love Him, you will love them. You will make them your dearest friends.

Reflection

Why is it so hard sometimes to love other Christians?

How can we cultivate such love among ourselves that those who don't know Christ will be drawn toward our love?

Boldly Bring Your Concerns to Jesus

"Let us therefore come boldly to the throne
of grace, that we may obtain mercy and find
grace to help in time of need."

Hebrews 4:16

Are you troubled? Go boldly to the throne of grace to obtain mercy and find grace to help in your time of need.

Are you bereaved of one you loved? Go and tell Jesus; spread out your sorrows at His feet. He knows them all, feels for you in them all. He is a merciful High Priest. He is faithful, too, always available in the hour of need. He is able to help you by His Word, by His Spirit, by His providence. He gave you all the comfort you received from your friends. He can give it to you without them. He has taken away the stream so that you may go to the fountain.

Are you suffering in body? Go to this High Priest. He is intimately acquainted with all your diseases; He has felt that very pain. Remember how, when they brought to Him one who was deaf and had a speech impediment, Jesus looked up to heaven, sighed, and said, "*Ephphatha*" (Mark 7:34). He sighed over the man's misery; likewise, He sighs over you. He is able to give you deliverance, patience to bear it, or improvement by it.

Are you sorely tempted in soul, put into trying circumstances so that you don't know what to do? Look up. He is able to help you. If He had been on the earth, would you not have gone to Him? Would you not have kneeled and said, "Lord, help me"? Does it make any difference that He is at the right hand of God? He is the same yesterday, today, and forever.

Reflection

Which challenges are you or a loved one facing today that you can bring to Jesus?

Has anything kept you from going to Him with your needs in the past?

If so, talk with Him about that, and turn to Him more quickly in the future.

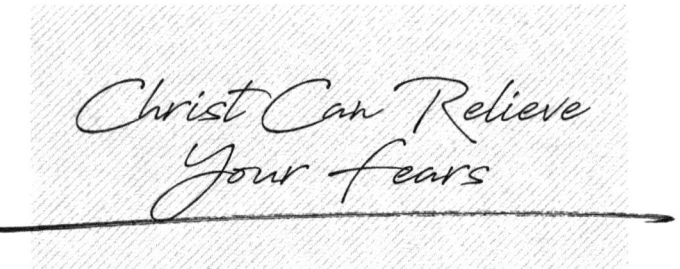

Christ Can Relieve Your Fears

"Perfect love casts out fear."

1 John 4:18

Here is good news for troubled, trembling souls. You do not need to live another hour under your tormenting fears. Jesus Christ has home the wrath of which you are afraid. He now stands as a refuge for the oppressed, a refuge in the time of trouble. Look to Christ, and your fear will be cast out. Come to the feet of Christ, and you will find rest. Call on the name of the Lord, and you will be delivered. You say, "I cannot look, nor come, nor cry, for I am helpless."

Hear, then, and your soul will live. Jesus is a Savior to the helpless. Christ is not only a Savior to those who are naked and empty and have no goodness to recommend themselves. He is also a Savior to those who are unable to give themselves to Him. You cannot be in too desperate a condition for Christ. As long as you remain unbelieving, you are under His perfect wrath. But the moment you look to Christ, you will come under His perfect love—love without any coldness, light without any shade, love without any cloud or mountain between. God's love will cast out all your fears.

Reflection

When fears arise,
what is your first
response?

What are you
fearful about today?

How can you give
those fears to God?

Ashamed of the Gospel

"I am not ashamed of the gospel of Christ,
for it is the power of God to salvation for
everyone who believes, for the Jew first and
also for the Greek."

Romans 1:16

Many people are ashamed of the gospel of Christ. The wise are ashamed of it because it calls men to believe and not to argue. The great are ashamed of it because it calls for humility and brings all equally into one body. The rich are ashamed of it because it is to be obtained without money and without price. The fun-loving are ashamed of it because they fear it will destroy all their mirth. So, all the good news of the glorious Son of God, Inning come into the world to rescue lost sinners, is despised. People are ashamed of it.

Which people are not ashamed of it? A little company—those whose hearts the Spirit of God has touched. They were once like the world and of it, but He awakened them to see their sin and misery. He revealed that Christ alone is a refuge. Now they cry, "None but Christ, none but Christ. God forbid that I should boast except in the cross of Christ." He is precious to their hearts; He lives there. He is often on their lips and praised in their families. They would gladly proclaim Him to all the world.

Dear friends, is this your experience? Have you

received the gospel, not in word only but in power? Has the power of God been put forth upon your soul along with the Word? Then this word is yours: I am not ashamed of the gospel of Christ.

Reflection

Why do some believers act ashamed of the gospel, ashamed to be called a Christian? Is your glory in the cross—or in other things?

Our Future Hope

"We shall be like Him, for we shall see Him as He is."

1 John 3:2

I t is the chief glory and joy of a soul to be like God. You remember that this was the glory of that condition in which Adam was created: "Let Us make man in Our image, according to Our likeness" (Gen. 1:26). Adam's understanding was without a cloud. He saw, in some measure, as God sees. Adam's will flowed in the same channel with God's will. Adam's affections fastened on the same objects that God also loved.

When man fell, we lost all this and became children of the Devil, not children of God. But when a lost soul is brought to Christ and receives the Holy Spirit, he puts off the old man and puts on the new man, which after God is created in righteousness and true holiness. It is our true joy in this world to be like God. Too many rest in the joy of being forgiven, but our truest joy is to be like Him. Rest not, beloved, until you are renewed after His image, until you partake of the divine nature. Long for the day when Christ will appear, and we will be fully like Him, for we will see Him as He is.

Reflection

Do you desire, every day, to become more like God?

What does it mean to "be renewed in His image"?

No Room in the Heart for Idols

"What have I to do anymore with idols?"

Hosea 14:8

I f you believe in Jesus, who justifies the ungodly, your faith is counted for righteousness. As long as you came to God in yourself, you were infinitely loathsome and condemned; mountains of iniquity covered your soul. But blessed be the Holy Spirit who has led you to Jesus. You have come to God's righteous Servant, who by His knowledge justifies many because He bears their iniquities. Your sins are covered; God sees no iniquity in you; God loves you freely; His anger is turned away from you. What have you to do anymore with idols? Is not the love of God enough for you?

The loving and much-loved wife is satisfied with the love of her husband; his smile is her joy, she cares little for any other. So, if you have come to Christ, His free love to you is all you need and all you care for. There is no veil between you and the Father. You have access to the fountain of happiness, of peace, of holiness. What have you to do anymore with idols? If your heart swims in the rays of God's love, you will have no room in your heart for idols.

Reflection

What kind of "idols" do people today worship?

How can you, with God's help, guard your heart and mind against all the idols of our culture?

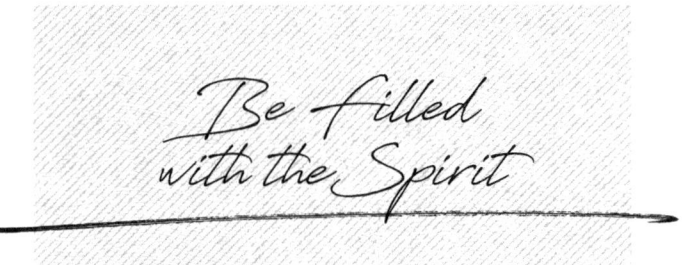

Be filled with the Spirit

"When he rose early the next morning and squeezed the fleece together, he wrung the dew out of the fleece, a bowlful of water."

Judges 6:38

I f this day you are united to Jesus, the Holy Spirit will come like dew upon your soul. The Spirit is given to those who obey Jesus. When all nature is at rest, not a leaf moving, then at evening the dew comes down, no eye to see the pearly drops descending, no ear to hear them falling on the verdant grass. So does the Spirit come to you who believe. When the heart is at rest in Jesus, unseen, unheard by the world, the Spirit comes and softly fills the believing soul, quickening all, renewing all within. "If I depart, I wall send Him to you" (John 16:7).

Dear little ones, whom God hath chosen out of this world, you are like Gideons fleece. The Lord will fill you with dew when all around is dry.

Reflection

Why do we need to
be constantly filled
with the Spirit?
How does He help
us when we are
struggling and
weary?

Salvation Is Given, Not Earned

"For by grace you have been saved through faith, and that not of yourselves; it is the gift of God, not of works, lest anyone should boast."

Ephesians 2:8–9

The misguided person seeks salvation by making himself better in the sight of God. He tries to mend his life. He puts a bridle on his tongue. He tries to command his feelings and thoughts, all to make himself better in the sight of God. Or he goes further. He tries to cover his past sins by religious observances. He becomes a religious man—prays, weeps, reads, attends sacraments, is deeply occupied in religion and tries to get it into his heart—all to make himself appear good in the eye of God so that he may obligate God to pardon and love him.

Paul tried this plan for a long time. He was a Pharisee, emphasizing blameless righteousness according to the law. He lived an outwardly blameless life and was highly thought of as a most religious man. "But what things were gain to me, these I have counted loss for Christ" (Phil. 3:7). When it pleased God to open Paul's eyes, he gave up this way of self-righteousness forever. He no longer had any peace from looking inward. "We . . . have no confidence in the flesh" (Phil. 3:3). He bade farewell forever to that way of seeking peace. No, he trampled it under his feet. "I . . . count them as rubbish, that I may gain Christ" (Phil 3:8).

Oh, it is a glorious thing when a man is brought to trample his own righteousness under his feet. It is the hardest thing in the world.

Reflection

Why do many people believe they must earn salvation through their own efforts? In what ways might you be trying to earn God's favor?

Joy in God's Presence

"O God, You are my God, early will I seek
You; my soul thirsts for You; my flesh longs
for You in a dry and thirsty land where there
is no water."

Psalm 63:1

An awakened soul feels that his chief happiness is in coming before God. This was the case with Adam before he sinned. He felt like a child under a loving father's eye. It was his chief joy to come before God, to be loved by Him, to be like a speck in the sunbeam, to bask continually in the sunshine of His love where no cloud or veil comes between. This is the joy of the holy angels, to come before the Lord and bow before the high God. In His presence is fullness of joy. "Their angels always see the face of My Father" (Matt. 18:10). On whatever errand of love they fly, they still feel that His eye of love is on them; this is their daily, hourly joy. This is the true happiness of a believer. Hear David: "As the deer pants for the water brooks, so pants my soul for You, O God. My soul thirsts for God, for the living God. When shall I come and appear before God" (Ps. 42:1-2)? He panted not after the gifts of God, not His favors or comforts, but after Himself.

A believer longs after God, to come into His presence, to feel His love, to feel near to Him in secret. Dear brethren, have you ever tasted this blessedness? There is greater rest and solace in God's presence for one hour than in an eternity in man's presence. To be in His presence, under His love, under His eye, is heaven wherever it is.

Reflection

Which activities or anxieties hinder you from coming into God's presence every day? How can you rest in His presence even when your schedule is hectic and so many demands are placed on you?

Let Your Praises Flow

"A woman came having an alabaster flask of
very costly oil of spikenard. Then she broke
the flask and poured it on His head."

Mark 14:3

Jesus had saved her soul, had saved her brother
and sister, and this woman felt that she could
not do too much for Him. She brought a costly
alabaster box of ointment, broke the box, and poured it
on His head. No doubt she loved His disciples— holy
John and frank Peter-—yet still she loved Christ more.
No doubt she loved Christ's poor and was often kind to
them, yet she loved Jesus more. On His blessed head that
would so soon be crowned with thorns, she poured the
precious ointment.

This is what we should do. If Christ has saved us, we
should pour out our best affections on Him. It is well to
love His disciples, His ministers, and His poor, but it's
best to love Him. We cannot now reach His blessed head,
but we can fall down at His footstool and pour out our
affections toward Him. It was not the ointment Jesus
cared for; what does the King of Glory care for a little
ointment? It is the loving heart poured out on His feet,
it is the adoration, praise, love, and prayers of a believer's
broken heart that Christ cares for. The new heart is the
alabaster box that Jesus loves.

Could you not give more time to pouring out your heart to Jesus—breaking the box and filling the room with the fragrance of your praise? Could you not pray more than you do to be filled with the Spirit, that the Spirit may be poured down on ministers, God's people, and an unconverted world?

Reflection

How much time do you spend praising God? Why do you think God desires your praise?

God's Awesome Strength

"Who is the King of glory? The Lord strong
and mighty."

Psalm 24:8

O ur God is all-powerful, and His strength is
scarcely comprehensible to us. How strong
is He? Consider:

God is stronger than Satan. Satan can no more hinder
God from carrying us to glory than a little fly can, which
you crush with your foot. He will "crush Satan under
your feet shortly" (Rom. 16:20). "Therefore submit to
God. Resist the devil and he will flee from you" (James
4:7).

God is stronger than the world. The world often comes
against us like armed men, but if God is for us, who can
be against us? Worldly men are a rod in God's hand.
God puts it this way or that way to fulfill all His pleasure;
and when He is done with it. He will break it into pieces
and cast it into the fire.

God is stronger than our hearts. There is many a Jericho
in our own hearts walled up to heaven, many a fortress
of sin, many giant lusts that threaten our souls. God
made the walls of Jericho fall flat by a mere breath of
wind—a noise. And He still can do this. Settle it in your

heart; there is no Jericho in your heart that God is not able to make fall in a moment. You have seen a shepherd earning a sheep on his shoulder. He meets with many stones on the way, many thorns, many streams, and yet the sheep feels no difficulty; it is carried above all. So it is with every soul that yields itself to God; the only difficulty is to lie on His shoulder.

Reflection

Which "Jerichos" have troubled you and need to be given to God?

What's the balance between taking action ourselves and having faith in our all-powerful and all-loving God to carry us through our difficulties?

Use Your Talents to Share Christ

"'You are My witnesses,' says the Lord, 'and My servant whom I have chosen.'"

Isaiah 43:10

The moment a man's eyes are opened to the value of his own soul, he begins to care for the souls of others. From that moment, he loves the missionary cause. He willingly spares a little to send the gospel to unbelieving peoples. Again, he begins to care for the church at home, for his neighbors, for all people living in sin.

When a man comes to Christ, he feels he is not his own (see 1 Cor. 6:19). He hears Christ say, "Occupy until I come." If he is rich, he uses all for Christ, like Gaius. If he is a learned man, he spends all for Christ, like Paul. If he is a gifted encourager, he heartens and cheers everyone he knows, like Barnabas.

How about you? What gifts and talents are you employing to shine the light of Christ in this darkened world?

Reflection

As you read this,
which persons came
to mind?

How willing are you
to share the love
and truth of Jesus
with people in your
spheres of
influence?

Choose Wisely

"Let us lay aside every weight, and the sin
which so easily ensnares us, and let us run
with endurance the race that is set before us."

Hebrews 12:1

Your journey to heaven should be your great concern. Dear friends, judge everything in this way, whether or not it will help you on your journey. In choosing a profession or trade, choose it with regard to this. Will it advance or hinder your heavenward journey? Will it lead you into strong temptations or into wicked company? Oh, take heed! What is the use of living, but only to get on in our journey to heaven?

Choose your abode with regard to this. Remember Lot. He chose the plain of Jordan because it was well watered, but his soul all but withered there.

In choosing connections or friends, choose with regard to this—will they help or hinder your prayers? Will they go with you and help you on your journey, or will they be a drag on your wheels?

In going into companies, in reading books, choose with regard to this. Will they fill your sails for heaven? If not, don't go near them. In yielding to your affections, especially if you find them hindering your journey, drop them instantly.

Reflection

What are some of the ways in which God guides us in making important choices?

How sensitive are you to His leading?

The Power of Holy Living

"God did not call us to uncleanness, but in holiness."

1 Thessalonians 4:7

The holiness of the believer is like the most precious perfume. When a holy believer goes through the world, filled with the Spirit, made more than conqueror, the fragrance fills the room "as if an angel shook his wings." If the world were full of believers, it would be like a bed of spices, but, oh, how few believers carry much of the odor of heaven along with them.

How many people might you be the means of saving if you lived a holy, consistent life—if you were evidently a sacrifice bound on Gods altar? Wives might, without the Word, win their husbands when they see your chaste conversation. Parents might in this way save their children, when they saw you holy and happy; children have often saved their parents. Servants, adorn the doctrine of God your Savior in all things; let your light shine before men. The poorest can do this as well as the richest, the youngest as well as the oldest. Oh, there is no argument like a holy life.

Reflection

What happens when
we don't live
consistently holy
lives?

Where does the
power to live a holy
life come from?

To Grow, Study Christ's Life

"Let us run with endurance the race that is set before us, looking unto Jesus, the author and finisher of our faith."

Hebrews 12:1-2

T he only way to hold fast is to believe more and more. Become better acquainted with Christ—with His person, work, and character. Every page of the gospel unfolds a new feature of His character; even line of the epistles discloses new depths of His work. Get more faith, and you will get a firmer hold. A plant that has a single root may be easily torn up by the hand, crushed by the foot of the wild beast, or blown down by the wind. But a plant that has a thousand roots struck down into the ground can stand.

Faith is like the root. Many people believe a little concerning Christ: one fact. Every new truth concerning Jesus is a new root struck downward. Believe more intensely. A root that is going in a right direction but not striking deep is easily torn up.

Pray for deep-rooted faith. Pray to be established, strengthened, and settled. Take a long, intense look at Jesus—often, often. If you wanted to remember a man again, and he was going away, you'd take an intense look at his face. Look then at Jesus—deeply, intensely—until every feature is engraved on your heart.

Reflection

What's the link between faith and studying the person, work, and character of Jesus?

What are some ways in which you can learn more about Him and develop a deeper relationship with Him?

Think Like Jesus

"We have the mind of Christ."

1 Corinthians 2:16

E very believer has the mind of Christ formed in him. He thinks as Christ does. "For God has not given us a spirit of fear, but of power and of love and of a sound mind" (2 Tim. 1:7). This is being of the same mind in the Lord. I do not mean that a believer has the same all-seeing mind, the same infallible judgment concerning everything that Christ has, but up to his light he sees things as Christ does.

He sees sin as Christ does. Christ sees sin to be evil and bitter, filthy and abominable, its pleasures all a delusion. He sees it to be awfully dangerous. He sees the inseparable connection between sin and suffering. So does the believer.

He sees the gospel as Christ does. Christ sees amazing glory in the gospel. The way of salvation that He Himself has wrought out. It appears to be a most complete salvation to Him, most free, most glorifying to God and happy for man. So does the believer.

He sees the world as Christ does. Christ knows what is in man. He looked on this world as vanity compared with the smile of His Father. Its riches, honors, and pleasures appeared to be not worth a sigh. He saw it passing away. So does the believer.

He sees time as Christ did. "I must work the works of Him who sent Me while it is day; the night is coming. Behold, I am coining quickly" (John 9:4; Rev. 3:11)! So does a believer look at time.

He sees eternity as Christ does. Christ looked at everything in the light of eternity. "In My Father's house are many mansions" (John 14:2). Everything is valuable in Christ's eyes, only as it hears on eternity. So with believers.

Reflection

Why is it so difficult to think like Jesus in this day and age? To what extent are you nurturing your mind to be the mind of Christ?

Proclaim the Good News

"Go therefore and make disciples of all the nations."

Matthew 28:19

I f you have really been brought to Christ and saved, you know there is a hell. You know that all the unconverted people around you are hurrying toward it. You know there is a Savior, and that He is stretching out His hands all day long to sinners. Could you do no more to save sinners than you do? Do you do all you can? You say that you pray for them, but is it not hypocrisy to pray and do nothing? Will God hear these prayers? Have you no fears that prayers without labors are only provoking God? You say that you can't speak, you aren't educated. Will that excuse stand at the judgment? Does it require much education to tell fellow sinners that they are perishing? If their houses were on fire, would it require much education to wake the sleepers?

Do you do what you can for your neighbors? Can you pass your neighbors for years, and see them on the broad way, without warning them? Could you not tell little children the way to be saved? Do you do what you can for the world?

Reflection

What are some ways, in your spheres of influence, in which you can both show and tell people about what Jesus has done for you?

Why is it important to pray for specific people and be willing to talk with them about God when He opens up opportunities to share His love and truth?

Pursue Discipline in Your Life

"Everyone who competes for the prize is
temperate in all things . . . I discipline my
body and bring it into subjection."

1 Corinthians 9:25, 27

It was long after his conversion that Paul wrote in this manner. He could say, "To me, to live is Christ, and to die is gain" (Phil. 1:21). He believed it would be better to depart and be with Christ. He knew there was a crown laid up for him, and yet we see how earnest he was to advance in the divine life. He was like one at the Grecian games running for a prize. This is the way all converted persons should seek salvation. It is common for many to sit down after conversion and say, "I am safe. I do not need to strive anymore." But Paul pressed toward the mark.

There was one particular area in which he was very earnest. "I discipline my body and bring it under subjection." He had observed during the Grecian games that those who were to run and fight were very attentive to this: "Everyone who competes for the prize is temperate in all things." Paul strove to be temperate in all things, especially in eating and drinking.

Reflection

In what ways do you
need more discipline
in your life?

How, specifically,
can you achieve a
more disciplined
lifestyle?

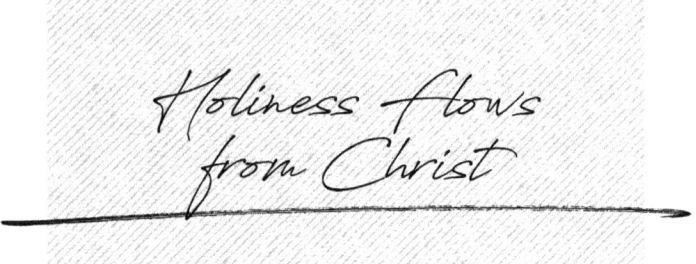

Holiness flows from Christ

"Christ also loved the church and gave Himself for her, that He might sanctify and cleanse her with the washing of water by the word, that He might present her to Himself a glorious church . . . holy and without blemish."

Ephesians 5:25-27

T rue holiness in this world springs from Christ. A living Christ is the spring of holiness to all His members. As long as we hold Him, and do not let Him go, our holiness is secure. He is engaged to keep us from falling. He loves us too well to let us fall under the reigning power of sin. His word is engaged: "I will put My Spirit within you" (Ezek. 36:27). His honor would be tarnished if any who cling to Him fall into sin.

You have no strength, no store of grace, no power to resist a thousand enemies. If Christ be for you, who can be against you? But if you let go of His arms, where are you?

Reflection

Why must we depend on Christ when sin lures us away from holiness?

What are some of the excuses you may be using to rationalize small or large sins that draw you away from Him?

Enjoy the World, but Do Not Love It

"The world is passing away, and the lust of it, but he who does the will of God abides forever."

1 John 2:17

I t is quite right for a believer to use the things of this world and to rejoice in them. No one has such a right as the believer to rejoice and he happy. He has a right to use the bodily comforts of this world, to eat his food "with gladness and simplicity of heart, praising God" (Acts 2:46-47). He has a right to all the joys of home, kindred, and friendship. It is highly proper that he should enjoy these things. He has a right to all the pure pleasures of mind, intellect, and imagination because God has given him all things richly to enjoy. Still, he should "use this world as not misusing it" (1 Cor. 7:31) because "the time is short" (v. 29).

In a little while, you'll be at your Father's table above. You'll meet with all your brothers and sisters in Christ. You'll have pure joy in God through ceaseless ages. Don't become greatly captivated with the joys that are here.

Reflection

How can you find the balance between enjoying earthly things God has provided, yet holding onto them loosely?

In contrast, what does our materialistic culture emphasize about earthly pleasures?

Servants, Here and Beyond

"Whatever you do, do it heartily, as to the
Lord and not to men."

Colossians 3:23

I t is right for Christians to he diligent in business.
They have good conscience that oils the wheels.
"A merry heart does good, like medicine" (Prov.
17:22). A light heart makes easy

They love to honor their Lord. They would not have
it said that a believer in Jesus was an idler or sluggard;
the love of Jesus compels them to all that is lovely. And
yet a believer should buy as though he doesn't possess
because "the time is short."

Oh, believers, you can't be misers because you are
but stewards. All that you possess here is your Lord's,
and the day is at hand when He will transfer you to take
care of another property in a brighter land. You are but
servants. It would not do if you were to set your hearts
on the things of this lower room because in a few days
the Master will call you to serve in Hi s own dear presence.

Be ready to leave your loom for the golden harp at
a minute's warning. Be reads to leas e your desk for the
throne of Jesus, your pen for the palm of victory. Be ready

to leave the market below for the street of the New Jerusalem where the redeemed will walk.

If you were in a sinking ship, sou wouldn't cling tightly to bags of money; you'd hold everything loosely and be ready to swim. This world is like a sinking ship, and those who grasp its possessions will sink with it.

Reflection

How is your "work ethic"? Why work hard on earth since our lives here are so temporary? What challenges does a person face today while working hard in business and striving to maintain focus on God and the heavenly life?

The Preciousness of Jesus

"In this you greatly rejoice . . . that the genuineness of your faith, being much more precious than gold that perishes, though it is tested by fire, may be found to praise, honor, and glory at the revelation of Jesus Christ."

1 Peter 1:6–7

Consider how precious Christ is. In Him is life eternal. In Him there is pardon for the vilest of sinners. In Him there is sweet peace of conscience—peace with God. In Him there is rest for the weary soul—the way to the Father—an open door into the fold of God. In Him there is a fountain of living waters—unsearchable riches—full supplies of grace and truth for weak and weary souls. In Him there is acquittal at the judgment day, and a glorious crown.

Oh, should you not leave everything for this? Will a lust, or a pleasure, or a game, or the smile of a friend keep you from all this? "Eye has not seen, nor ear heard, nor have entered into the heart of man the things which God has prepared for those who love Him" (1 Cor. 2:9).

Reflection

Thank Jesus today
for all that He has
done for you and the
blessed hope in store
for every believer.

Allow His peace,
hope, love, and joy to
permeate your life
and your interactions
with other people:
family members,
friends, neighbors,
and coworkers.

A Much Better Banquet Awaits Us

"The form of this world is passing away."

1 Corinthians 7:31

I have noticed that children, when they were going out to a feast, eat sparingly so that they might have a keener appetite for the coming desserts. Likewise, dear friends, you are going to a feast above. Don't dull your appetite with earthly joys. Hold them loosely, looking upon them as fading. As you walk-through a flower garden, you never think of King down to make your home among its roses, so pass through the garden of this world's best joys. Smell the flowers in passing, but do not tarry. Jesus calls you to His banqueting house, where you will feed among the lilies on the mountains of spices. Oh, it ill becomes a child of God to be fond of an earthly banquet when you will be sitting down quite soon with Jesus. It ill becomes you to be greatly preoccupied with dress and show when you will so soon see the face that was crowned with thorns.

Brethren, if you are ever so deeply taken up with any enjoyment that it takes away your love for prayer or for your Bible, or that it would frighten you to hear the cry, "The bridegroom comes" and you'd reply, "Has He come already?" then you are abusing this world.

Reflection

Are any earthly pleasures sidetracking you from knowing God better?

Is anything consuming your thoughts and energies so that you have little time for Bible reading and prayer?

If so, ask God to help you find proper balance in your life.

Nothing Can Separate You from God's Love

"I am persuaded that neither death nor life, nor angels nor principalities nor powers, nor things present nor things to come, nor height nor depth, nor any other created thing, shall be able to separate us from the love of God which is in Christ Jesus our Lord."

Romans 8:38-39

Many of you may he cast down and your souls disquieted. You think God has dealt bitterly with you. He has allowed you to be childless; He has met you as a lion and as a bear bereaved of her cubs. He has withered your shady plant (see Jonah 4:5-7) or deserted you so that you seek Him and don't find Him.

Look still to Jesus. The love of God shines on Him, and nothing can separate Jesus from that love—and separate you from it. Your afflictions and desertions only prove that you are under the Father's hand. There is no time when the patient is an object of such tender interest to the surgeon as when he is under his knife. So, you may be sure that if you are suffering from the hand of God, His eve is all the more focused on you. "The eternal God is your refuge, and underneath are the everlasting arms" (Dent. 33:27).

Invite poor sinners to come and taste of this love. It is a sweet thing to be loved. I suppose that most of you have tasted a mother's love. You know' what it is to be rocked in her arms, to he watched In her gentle eve, to be cheered by her smile. But, brethren, this is nothing compared to the love of your God. That dear mother's eve will close in death; that dear mother's arm will decay in the dust. Oh, come and share the love of Him who cannot die. Abide in Him, and that love will abide in you.

Reflection

Do you fully realize the depth of God's love for you, or comprehend how much He cares for you even though right now it may not seem as if He does? Why is it sometimes difficult for us to understand the depth of God's love?

Praise God in Unity

"Sing praises to God, sing praises! Sing
praises to our King, sing praises!"

Psalm 47:6

D ear children of God, unite your praises. Let
your hearts no more he divided. You are
divided from the world by a great gulf. Soon
it will be an infinite gulf, but you are united to one another by the same Spirit. You have been chosen by the
same free, sovereign love. You have been washed in the
same precious blood. You have been filled by the same
blessed Spirit. Little children, love one another. He who
loves is born of God.

Be one in your praises. Join in one cry, "Worthy is the
Lamb who was slain" (Rev. 5:12). Oh, be fervent in praise.
Lift up your voices in it; lift up your hearts in it. In heaven,
they wax louder and louder. John heard the sound of a
great multitude; it was like many waters, and then it was
like mighty thunderings, crying, "Alleluia" (Rev. 19:6).

I remember Edwards' remark that it was in the singing
of praises that his people felt themselves most enlarged,
and then that God was worshipped somewhat in the
beauty of holiness. Let it be so among yourselves. Learn,
dearly beloved, to praise God heartily, to sing with all
your heart and soul in the family and in the congregation.

Reflection

What exactly does it mean for believers to "unite their praises"?

What prevents this from happening?

For what kinds of things can you praise God today?

The Spirit Helps Us Move Forward

"The Helper, the Holy Spirit, whom the
Father will send in My name, He will teach
you all things, and bring to your
remembrance all things that I said to you."

John 14:26

A re there not some of you who have come to
Christ and nothing more? Guilty, weary,
heavy laden, you have found rest, redemption
through His blood, and even the forgiveness of sins. Oh,
do not stop there. Do not rest in mere forgiveness; cry
for the indwelling of the Holy Spirit, the Comforter.
Forgiveness is but a means to an end. You are justified
in order that you may be sanctified. Remember, without
holiness you will never see the Lord, and without this
indwelling Spirit you never will be holy.

Aren't some of you groaning under a body of sin and
death, crying with the apostle, "O wretched man that I
am! Who will deliver me from this body of death" (Rom.
7:24)? Do you not feel the plague of your heart? Do you
not feel the power of your old nature? How many people
in this state lean on themselves, trusting in their resolutions, attempting, as it were, by force, to put down their
sins? Here is the remedy. Oh, cry for the floodtide of
God's Spirit, that He may fill every chamber of your
heart, that He may renew you in the spirit of your mind.

Are there not many who are cold, worldly Christians,

those who were long ago converted, but have fallen sadly back under the power of the world—either its gaiety or its business, its mirth or its money—and they have gotten into worldly habits, deep ruts of sin? See what you need. He who created man in His own image, at first, must create you over again. You need an almighty, indwelling Comforter. Only He can melt your icy heart and make it flow out in los e to God, who can fill you with all His fullness.

Reflection

Are you being refreshed by the Holy Spirit every day, or are you feeling trapped in sin and stale in faith?

In what ways might the Spirit help you grow and move forward in the year ahead?

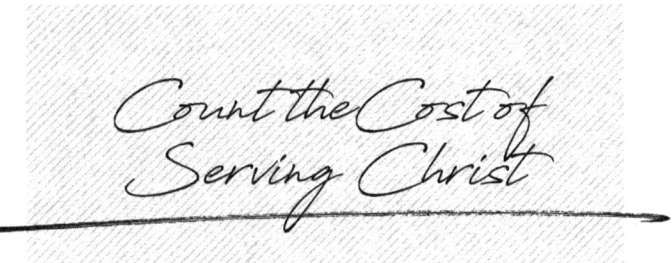

Count the Cost of Serving Christ

"Whoever does not bear his cross and come after Me cannot be My disciple. For which of you, intending to build a tower, does not sit down first and count the cost, whether he has enough to finish it."

Luke 14:27-28

If we would be Christ's, we must give up ourselves to His service forever. The Greeks said, "Sir, we wish to see Jesus" (John 12:21). Jesus told them that a mere sight of Him would not do: "If anyone serves Me, let him follow Me" (John 12:26).

Many people are willing to be saved from hell, but they are unwilling to give themselves up to Christ to be His servants and followers. But every person who is under the teaching of the Spirit gives himself up to be the Lord's. Consider Matthew. The Lord said, "'Follow Me.' So he arose and followed Him" (Matt. 9:9).

One who is truly taught by God feels indwelling sin to be a greater burden than the fear of hell: "In me (that is, in my flesh) nothing good dwells" (Rom. 7:18). Therefore, that soul is willing to be Christ's servant forever—willing to have his ear next to the door of Christ's house.

This will reveal hypocrites. Are you willing to be Christ's servant, to follow Him in fulfilling hard duties, to be brought under the rules of the gospel? If not, you are guilty of hypocrisy. Count the cost of coming to Christ.

Reflection

What does in mean
to "count the cost"
of serving Christ in
our everyday lives?

Are there any areas
of your life in which
you are not
following Jesus?

A Mighty Fortress

"You are my rock and my fortress."

Psalm 31:3

I f sinners only knew the Person who has undertaken to be a Savior, it would dispel all their fears. He is the brightness of Gods glory and the express image of His person. He is the peerless, matchless Son of God who has undertaken to stand for us. He is the maker of the world, who sees the end from the beginning. "All things were made through Him" (John 1:3). He made the sun, moon, and stars. He made the solid earth. He upholds all things by the word of His power.

Do you think He would fail in any undertaking? Do you think, if He engages to be a fortress for believers, that he will not be enough to protect them? Oh, be ashamed of your unbelief and find shelter within this stronghold. "Behold, God is my salvation, I will trust and not be afraid" (Isa. 12:2). Come under this Rock, and you will find rest for your weary souls. It matters not which sins you have. If you come under Christ, you will have peace.

Reflection

Are you trusting Jesus to handle the difficult challenge(s) you are facing?

Meditate on His love for you, the trust He longs for you to have in Him, and the salvation He offers.

God Helps Us Withstand Temptation

I have no doubt that Noah often said, "I fear that I, too, will be carried away by the flood. I fear my faith will fail me. I don't know what to do." And Lot often trembled in Sodom, as did David when Saul pursued him.

Many of you don't know how to deliver yourselves. You are surrounded as with a flood: old companions, old lusts, a hating world, a roaring lion. Man doesn't know how to deliver you. Nothing is more vain than the help of man during an hour of temptation.

The Lord knows. More is meant that these mere words imply. The Lord not only knows how to do it but will certainly deliver the godly out of temptation. He loves them. Every godly person is a jewel in His sight. He died for them, and He will not lose one. When He puts them into the furnace, He sits as a refiner. He has promised to stand beside you always: "He will not leave you nor forsake you" (Deut. 31:8).

It matters not what the temptation is, how great the temptation is, and how weak the believing soul is. Some children of God say sometimes, "If it were a lesser trial, I could bear it. If the furnace were not so hot, if the temptation were not so great, I could get through." Or, "If only I had more strength, if I were an older and more experienced believer." Look at these words: "The Lord knows how to deliver the godly out of temptations." Is anything too hard for the Lord?

Reflection

Which temptations tend to dog you?
In light of this reading, how might you respond differently when the next temptations come?

Faultless in God's Righteousness

"Now to Him who is able to . . . present you
faultless before the presence of His glory."

Jude v. 24

As long as you live in your mortal body, you will be faulty in yourself. It is a soul-mining error to believe anything else. If you would become wise, often look beneath the robe of the Redeemers righteousness to see your deformity. It will make you keep tighter hold of His robe and keep you washing in the fountain.

When Christ brings you before the throne of God, He will clothe you with His fine linen and present you faultless. What a glorious righteousness that can stand the light of God's face! Sometimes a garment appears white in dim light, but when you bring it into the sunshine you see the spots. Prize, then, this divine righteousness, which is your covering.

My heart sometimes sickens when I think of the defects of believers—when I think of one Christian being fond of carousing, another vain, another given to evil speaking. Aim to be holy Christians—bright, shining Christians. The heavens are more adorned by the large, bright constellations than by many insignificant stars, so God may be more glorified by one bright Christian than by many indifferent ones. Aim at being that one.

We will be faultless. He who began will perform it. We will be like Him, for we will see Him as He is. When you lay down this body, you may say, "Farewell lust forever, farewell my hateful pride, farewell hateful self-ishness, farewell strife and envying, farewell being ashamed of Christ." This makes death sweet indeed. Long to depart and be with Christ.

Reflection

To what extent are you aware of your sinfulness? How committed are you to shining the light of Christ through holy living?

Share Your Resources Willingly

"Inasmuch as you did not do it to one of the least of these, you did not do it to Me."

Matthew 25:45

I f you have felt the love of God, you must dash down the idol of money. You must not love money. You must be more openhearted, more openhanded. You must give more to missions, to send the knowledge of Jesus to the Jews and to the Gentile world. Oh. how can you grasp your money in hand so greedily while there are hundreds of millions perishing? You who give tens must give your hundreds. You who are poor must do what you can. Remember Mary and the widows mites (see Mark 12:41-44). Let us resolve to give the tenth of all we have to God. "God is able to make all grace abound toward you, that you, always having all sufficiency in all things, may have an abundance for every good work" (2 Cor. 9:8).

Reflection

If you were to study your checkbook and bank accounts, what would it reveal about how you spend money?

What keeps many Christians from truly being openhanded and open-hearted?

Compelled by Christ's Love

"To this end I also labor, striving according
to His working which works in me mightily."

Colossians 1:29

W ho would not desire to hear from Paul's lips the mighty principle that sustained him through so many toils and dangers? What magic spell had taken possession of this mighty mind? What unseen planetary influence, with unceasing power, drew him on through all the discouragements, indifferent to the world's dread laugh and the fear of man that brings a snare, to the sneer of the skeptical Athenian, the frown of the luxurious Corinthian, and the rage of the narrow-minded Jew? What said the apostle? "The love of Christ compels us" (2 Cor. 5:14).

That Christ's love to man is here intended, and not our love to the Savior, is quite obvious from the explanation that follows, where His dying for all is pointed to as the example of His love. It was Paul's view of that strange compassion of the Savior—moving Him to die for His enemies, to bear double for all our sins, to taste death for every man—that gave Paul the impulse in every labor, which made all suffering light to him, every commandment not grievous. He ran with patience the race that was set before him. Why? Because, looking toward Jesus, he lived as a man crucified to the world and the world crucified to him. By what means? By looking to the cross of Christ.

As the natural sun in the heavens exercises a mighty and unceasing attractive energy on the planets that circle around it, so did the Sun of Righteousness, which had arisen on Paul with a brightness above that of noonday, exercise on his mind a continual and almighty energy, compelling him to live henceforth no more to himself, but to Him who died for him and rose again,

Christ's love compelled Paul, It was the ever-present, ever-abiding, ever-moving power that formed the main-spring of all his working.

Reflection

What, or who, compels you? To what extent are you motivated by and depending on Christ and His love?

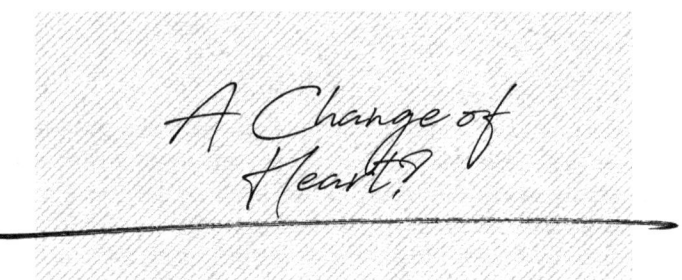

A Change of Heart?

"The heart is deceitful above all things, and desperately wicked; who can know it?"

Jeremiah 17:9

A man may be able to change his sins, but, ah, what man can change his heart? The reason why this is so utterly impossible with man is that he is not only fond of the objects of sin, he is fond of his sinful heart. He is not only indulgent, but he loves his indulgence. He is not only scornful, but delights in scorning. He is not only a fool, but he hates the very knowledge that would make him wise unto salvation.

There is only one remedy for the corrupt heart: the willing surrender to the Spirit of God.

Reflection

How does God's view of the heart differ from what people today often say about human goodness?

Why is God the only one who can spiritually transform the human heart?

We Battle Satan, but Victory Is Certain

"We do not wrestle against flesh and blood,
but against principalities, against powers,
against the rulers of the darkness of this
age, against spiritual hosts of wickedness in
the heavenly places."

Ephesians 6:12

A n awakened soul often has an awful warfare with Satan. Satan fights against him in two ways: first, by stirring up his depravity and making his lusts to flame and burn within him in a fearful manner, and second, by accusing him. Satan is the accuser of the brethren. He accuses the soul in his conscience in order to drive him away from Christ, drive him to despair, and give up all hope of salvation. Satan says to him, "You are a vile wretch, not fit for a holy Savior. See what raging lusts are in your heart; you will never be saved."

Ah, when the poor sinner runs to Christ, he finds rest there; his warfare is then accomplished. He sees all the accusations of Satan answered in the blood of the Lamb. Indeed, in one sense the battle is not over, but just beginning, but now victory is sure. God is now for him. Greater is He who is for him than all that can be against him. "If God is for us, who can be against us?" (Rom. 8:31). The Spirit of God is now within him and will abide with him forever. The Spirit now reigns in him. Christ now fights for him, covers his head during the day of battle, and carries him on His shoulder. He is as sure to overcome as if he were already in glory.

God says to him, "I will never leave you nor forsake you" (Heb. 13:5). That phrase, "never leave you," reaches through the darkest hours of temptation, the deepest waters of affliction, the hottest fires of persecution; it reaches until death, through death and the grave, and into eternity.

Reflection

Why is it so important to remember that Christ has overcome Satan and that we don't have to fight our spiritual battles on our own?

In which areas do you particularly need God's help today?

In faith, focus on Jesus

"My eyes are ever toward the Lord."

Psalm 25:15

I t is too true that believers sin, but it is just as true that unbelief is the cause of their sinning. If, brethren, you and I were to live with our eyes so closely on Christ that we had constant assurance of His overwhelming love for us and His almighty power within us, then, frail and helpless as we are, we should never sin. We should not have the slightest object in sinning.

But, my friends, how often during the day is Christ's love quite out of view! How often is it obscured to us, sometimes hidden from us by God Himself to teach us what we are. Who can wonder, then, that where there is so much unbelief, dread and hatred of God should again and again creep in, and sin should often display its poisonous head? The matter is clear if only we had spiritual eyes to see it. If we live a life of faith on the Son of God, we will assuredly live a life of holiness. Insofar as we do not live a life of faith, we will live a life of unholiness. It is through faith that God purifies the heart; there is no other way.

Reflection

What can you do today to focus more on Jesus?

Which things in particular tempt you to love the carnal world's temporary "delights"?

Where has unbelief taken hold in your life?

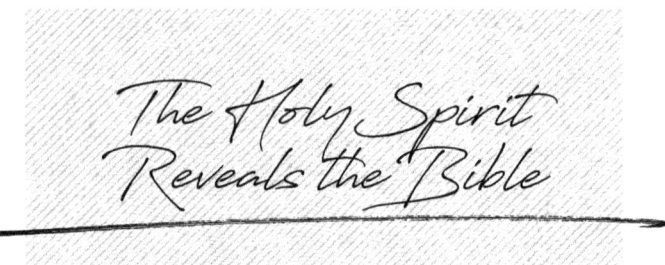

The Holy Spirit Reveals the Bible

"Sanctify them by Your truth. Your word is truth."

John 17:17

Are there not some who read the Bible, but get little from it? You feel that it does not sink into your heart, does not remain with you through the week. It is like the seed cast in the wayside, easily plucked away.

It is an outpoured Spirit whom you require to hide the Word in your heart. When you write with a dry pen, without any ink in it, no impression is made upon the paper. Now, God's people are the pens, and the Spirit of God is the ink. Pray that the pen may he filled with that living ink, that the Word may remain in your hearts, known and read by all men—that you may be sanctified through the truth.

Reflection

Does God's Word
stick with you after
you read it?

Ask the Holy Spirit
to fill you anew, to
enable you to retain
more of God's
Word and be made
more like Christ
through its powerful
truth.

We Are God's Workmanship

"We are His workmanship, created in Christ Jesus for good works, which God prepared beforehand that we should walk in them."

Ephesians 2:10

Remember, in the book of Revelation, how often Jesus says," I know your works." He says it with delight in the case of Smyrna: "I know your works, tribulation, and poverty (but you are rich)" (Rev. 2:9). When God brings a soul into Christ, He makes him a new creature, then God loves the new creature. Just as when God made the world. He saw all that He had made, and smiled because all was very good, so, when God makes a new creation in the heart, He delights in it. He says it is all very good.

God loves His own workmanship. His Spirit prays in you, lives in you, and walks in you. God loves the work of His Spirit. Just as you love flowers you have planted, as you love a garden spot on which you have focused much attention, so God loves His children, not for anything of their own but for what He has done for them and in them. They are dearly bought; He has bought them with His own blood. He waters them every moment, lest anyone hurt them. He keeps them by night and by day, and how can He but love them? He loves the place where His Spirit dwells.

God makes a Christian bear fruit and loves the work of His own hands. Dear Christians, walk after the Spirit and please God more and more. He saves those who have a contrite spirit. His face beholds the upright.

Reflection

What does it mean to "walk after the Spirit"?
Why is it essential to remember that you are Gods workmanship?

Renewed from the Inside Out

"Create in me a clean heart, O God, and
renew a steadfast spirit within me."

Psalm 51:10

By nature we love sin, the world, and the things of the world, although we know that the wages of sin is death. Now, to cure this I can imagine a man setting himself down deliberately to cross all his corrupted passions, to restrain all his appetites, to reject and trample on all the objects that the natural heart is set upon. This is the very system recommended by Satan, anti-Christ, and the world.

But there is a far more excellent way, which the Holy Spirit makes use of in sanctifying us—not the way of changing the objects, but the way of changing the affections; not by external restraint, but by an internal renewing. As is said in Ezekiel: "I will give them one heart, and I will put a new spirit within them, and take the stony heart out of their flesh, and give them a heart of flesh, that they may walk in My statutes and keep My judgments and do them" (11:19-20).

If anyone has been deceived by the detestable heresy of the world—as if the keeping of the commandments by the saints were a grievous and unwilling service—let that person open his eyes to the true nature of holiness.

God does not offer to work in you to do, without first working in you to will. He does not offer to pluck from you your favorite objects, but He offers to give you a new taste for higher objects. Just as the boy finds it no hardship to cast away toys and trifles that were his best friends in childhood, so the saint feels no hardship in casting away wretched playthings that so long amused and cheated the soul. Behold, the Spirit of God has opened up a new world to the admiring, enamored gaze of the believer in Jesus.

Reflection

How is a "renewed heart" demonstrated in everyday life? Have you asked God to give you a "new heart," to give you the will to pursue holiness in the Spirits power?

Two Very Different Feasts

"He, bearing His cross, went out to a place called the Place of a Skull, which is called in Hebrew, Golgotha, where they crucified Him."

John 19:17-18

Anxious souls, the people of this world try to cheer you. They invite you to be in their company, enjoy pleasure, drive away dull thoughts, and divert attention from important matters. They spread a feast for you in an opulent hall, where wine and rich foods are proffered. Every effort is made to encourage revelry and merrymaking. Oh, anxious soul, flee these things. Remember Lot's wife. If you are anxious about your soul, flee from the feasts of the world.

God also prepares a feast, but where? On Calvary. There is no light; it is all darkness around the cross. There is no music, only the groan of a dying Savior: "*Eli! Eli! . . .* My God! My God!" (Matt. 27:46). Anxious soul, it is there you will find peace and rest. "Come to Me, all you who labor and are heavy laden, and I will give you rest" (Matt. 11:28). The darkest hour that ever was in this world gives light to the weary soul. The sight of the cross brings us within sight of the crown. That dying sigh, which made the rocks rend, alone can give you peace. The Place of a Skull is the place of joy.

Reflection

Compare the "feasts" offered by the world and by God.

What did Jesus accomplish through His death and resurrection that enables believers to experience joy and peace with God and, one day, eternal life?

Temporary Troubles, Lasting Glory

"Our light affliction, which is but for a
moment, is working for us a far more
exceeding and eternal weight of glory."

2 Corinthians 4:17

The dangers to which the believer is exposed are but for a time. It was so during that night when God smote the firstborn in Egypt. It was but a night that His people were to hide in their houses: "None of you shall go out of the door of his house until morning" (Ex. 12:22). It was so during the destruction of Jericho; Rahab and her kindred hid themselves seven days until the danger was past.

Temporal troubles are but for a moment; these sad sicknesses and wasting calamities will not last forever. A short while, and this body will be past the power of pain to grieve it. I know that if any of you have tasted the sweetness of being in Christ, you could be content to hide in Him for an eternity. Live but a few more years in faith, and you will live the rest in glory. "If we endure, we shall also reign with Him" (2 Tim. 2:12).

Reflection

Why is it so difficult sometimes to remember the truth of this reading, especially when we are experiencing great trouble?

How can we gain a more eternal, rather than temporal, perspective of hardship and pain?

Many People Refuse to Be Rescued

"But you are not willing to come to Me that you may have life."

John 5:40

T here's nothing more sad and strange than when there is a Savior who is enough for all the world, yet so few come to Him to be saved. If a lifeboat were sent out to a shipwreck, sufficient to save all the crew members, and if it came back with fewer than half of them, you would ask anxiously why the rest had not been saved by it. Likewise, when Christ has come to seek and save those who are lost, it behooves us to inquire why so many are not saved by Him. We have the answer in the verse above. Some people may be unaware of Christ's power to save them; far more acknowledge His power but simply refuse to receive the gift. They are not willing to come to Him.

The whole Bible shows that Christ is quite sufficient to save all the world, that all the world would be saved if all the world were to come to Him. "Behold! The Lamb of God who takes away the sin of the world" (John 1:29)! The meaning of this is not that the sins of the whole world have now been taken away. It is quite plain that the whole world is not forgiven at present because the whole world is not saved; because God everywhere calls sinners to repentance, and the first work of the Holy Spirit is to convince of sin, because forgiveness in the Bible is everywhere attached to believing.

Reflection

What do people in today's culture believe will get them to heaven?

How concerned are you for people who do not yet have a personal relationship with God through Jesus?

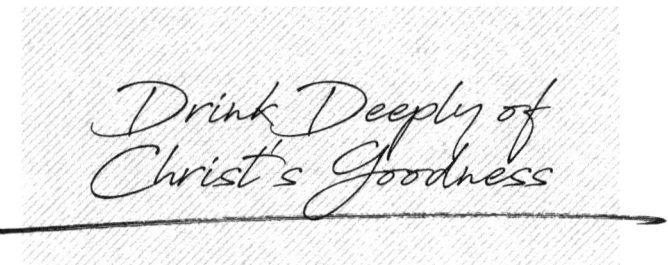

Drink Deeply of Christ's Goodness

"If anyone thirsts, let him come to Me and drink."

John 7:37

O

h, how many people seem to come to Jesus and yet don't drink! How few Christians are like a tree planted by the rivers of water. What would you have thought of the Jews if they had refused to drink when Moses struck the rock (see Num. 20:11)? Or what would you have thought if they had only put the water to their lips? Yet such is the way with many Christians.

It pleased the Father that in Christ all fullness should dwell. The Holy Spirit was given to Him without measure. The command is given to us to draw out of His fullness, yet who obeys? Not one in a thousand.

A Christian in our day is like a man who has a great reservoir filled with water. He is at liberty to drink as much as he pleases because he never can drink it dry. But instead of drinking the full stream that flows from it, he dams it up and is content to drink the few drops that trickle through. Oh that you who have come to Christ would draw out of His fullness! Don't be misers of grace. There is far more than you wall use in eternity. The same waters are now in Christ that refreshed Paul, that gave Peter his boldness, that gave John his affectionate tenderness. W in is your soul less richly supplied than theirs? Because you will not drink.

If you will come to Jesus and drink, you will become a fountain; you will be changed into the image of Christ. Through your heart, through your words, and through your prayers, the stream of grace will flow into other hearts.

Reflection

What does it mean, specifically, to "drink deeply" of Christ's goodness and power?
Are you drinking deeply or grabbing a few sips from time to time?

Freedom from Guilt

"If we walk in the light as He is in the light,
we have fellowship with one another, and the
blood of Jesus Christ His Son cleanses us
from all sin."

1 John 1:7

W hen a man is under a debt, if he pays it then he is free from the debt. So Christ was King under our sins, but He suffered all the punishment and now is free. He rose, and we see Him no more.

There is freedom from all guilt in Christ. He is quite free; He will never suffer anymore. He is without sin, and when He comes again He will be coming without sin. If you will become one with Him, you also will be free from guilt. You will be as free as Christ is. You will be as safe from being punished as if you were in heaven with Christ.

If you believe in Jesus, you are one with Him—a member of His body. And as sure as Christ your Savior has passed from the darkness of God's anger into the light of His countenance, so surely have you, believer, passed from darkness into God's marvelous light.

Reflection

Are you bolding on
to guilt as the result
of some sin you
think God won't
forgive?

Confess your sins to
Him and receive His
complete
forgiveness.

Don't Just Know about God, Experience Him

"Oh, taste and see that the Lord is good."

Psalm 34:8

There is all the difference in the world between knowing a thing and feeling a thing—between having a knowledge of a thing and having a sense of it. There is all the difference in the world between knowing that honey is sweet and tasting that it is sweet in order to have a sense of its sweetness. There is a great difference between knowing that a person is beautiful and actually seeing in order to have a present sense of the person's beauty. There is a great difference between knowing that a glove will fit the hand and putting the glove on in order to have a sense of its fitness.

Likewise, brethren, there is all the difference between having a head knowledge of Christ and His righteousness and having a heart feeling of His fitness and preciousness. The first may be acquired from flesh and blood, or from books; the second must come from the Spirit of God.

The Devil plainly has much knowledge of the Bible. From the quotations he made to Christ, it is plain that he understood much of the work of redemption. Yet he is none the better for it; he only trembles and gnashes his teeth more. Ah, my friends, if you have no more than head knowledge of Christ and His righteousness, you have no more than the Devil's.

Reflection

What happens when
we elevate head
knowledge of God
instead of actually
experiencing Him
with our hearts and
minds?

What are the
limitations of
knowing God only
with our minds?

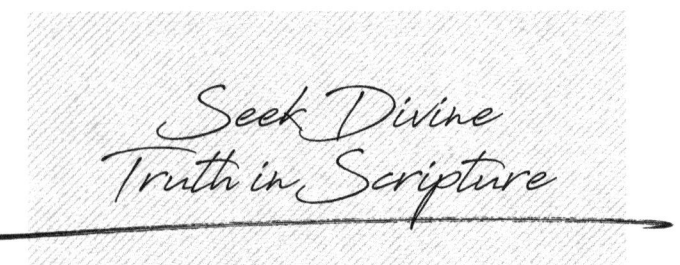

Seek Divine Truth in Scripture

"Your word I have hidden in my heart, that I might not sin against You. Blessed are You, O Loud! Teach me Your statutes."

Psalm 119:11-12

When the Spirit revealed Christ to the apostles and prophets of old. He revealed new truths concerning Christ. But when He convinces a sinner of Christ's righteousness, He does it by opening up the truths contained in the Bible. If He revealed new truths, then we might put away the Bible and sit alone, waiting for the Spirit to come down on us. But this is contrary to the Bible and experience.

David prayed. "Open my eyes, that I may see wondrous things" (Ps. 119:18). Where? Not in heaven above or earth beneath, but "from Your law." It is through the truth that the Spirit always works in our hearts. "Sanctify them by Your truth. Your word is truth" (John 17:17).

Therefore, when you look for conviction of righteousness, you are not to look for new truths not in the Bible, but for the divine light cast upon old truths already in the Bible.

Reflection

Why, in light of all the spiritual philosophies and ideas of our culture today, are the words of this reading relevant?

What insight from Scripture have you learned recently?

Keep Your Eyes on Christ

"And when Peter had come down out of the
boat, he walked on the water to go to Jesus."

Matthew 14:29

I f you are visited with seasons of coldness and indifference, if you begin to be weary or lag behind in the service of God, behold! Here is the remedy: fix your eyes firmly and waveringly on the Savior. That Sun of Righteousness is the grand shining center around which all His saints move swiftly and in smooth, harmonious concert. As long as the believing eye is fixed on His love, the path of the believer is easy and unimpeded because that love always compels. But lift off the believing eye, and the path becomes impracticable, the life of holiness a weariness.

Whoever, then, would live a life of persevering holiness, let him keep his eye continually on the Savior. As long as Peter looked only toward the Savior, he walked on the sea in safety, going toward Jesus. But when he looked around and saw the boisterous wind, he was afraid and, beginning to sink, cried, "Lord, save me" (Matt. 14:30)!

Just so will it be with you. As long as you look believingly to the Savior, who loved you and gave Himself for you, you may tread the waters of life's troubled sea, and the soles of your feet will not be wet. But venture to look around at the winds and waves that threaten you on every hand and, like Peter, you will begin to sink and cry, "Lord, save me!"

Reflection

When difficulties arise, why is it so hard to keep focused on Jesus?

What types of things cause you to take your attention off Jesus?

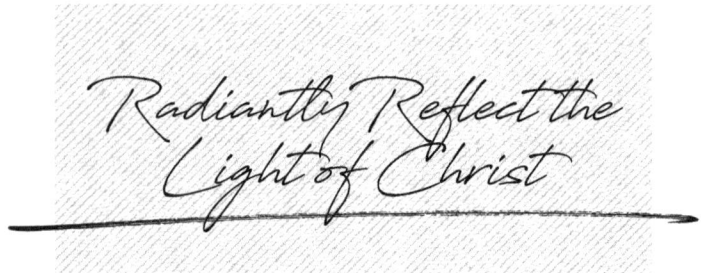

Radiantly Reflect the Light of Christ

"A city that is set on a hill cannot be hidden."

Matthew 5:14

Christian set on God's holy hill cannot he hidden. No man lights a candle and puts it under a bushel or a bed; he puts it on a candlestick. Then it gives light to all who are in the house.

Christians are to become like Christ—little suns who rise and shine on the dark world. He arises and shines on us and then says to us, "Arise, shine." This is Christs command to all for whom He has arisen: "Arise, shine."

Dear Christians, you are the lights of the world. Poor, feeble, dark, and sinful though you be. Be like the sun that shines every day and in every place. Wherever Jesus goes, He carries light; so do you. Some shine like the sun in public before men, but are dark as night in their own families. Dear Christians, look more to Christ, and you will shine more constantly.

Shine with Christs light. The moon rises and shines, but not with her own light. She gathers all from the sun. So do you. Shine in such a way that Christ will have all the glory. They shine brightest who most deeply feel their own darkness and are most clothed in Christs brightness. Oh, wherever you go, make it known that your light and peace all come from Him. It is by looking to Jesus that you shine. Your holiness conies from union with Him.

Reflection

How well are you reflecting the light of Christ to your family, friends, coworkers, and neighbors?
What will keep your light shining brightly?

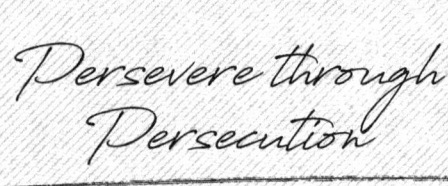

Persevere through Persecution

"After eight days His disciples were again inside, and Thomas with them. Jesus came, the doors being shut, and stood in the midst, and said, 'Peace to you!'"

John 20:26

The disciples had shut the doors of their upper room for fear of the Jews. The disciples were reproached and vilified as those who had been with Christ. There was some fear that they would he forced to share the same death, so they shut the doors of the place where they met. But at that very time, Jesus chose to enter. When the world was threatening them, saying, "Torments and death to you," Jesus said, "Peace to you."

So it is now. The world is just as bitter against Christians now as it ever was. Some of you have become partakers of the afflictions of the gospel and are feeling that the offense of the cross has not ceased. Worldly friends may upbraid, persecute, and reproach you, but never mind. Christs voice, though it is a still, small voice, is yet far louder than all the world. It calmed the waves of the Sea of Galilee, and it will speak peace to your soul. When the waves of persecution roar against you, He says, "Don't be afraid. It is I. Peace to you."

Reflection

Why are many people against Christians in our day and age?

How do you respond when people criticize you for your faith in Christ?

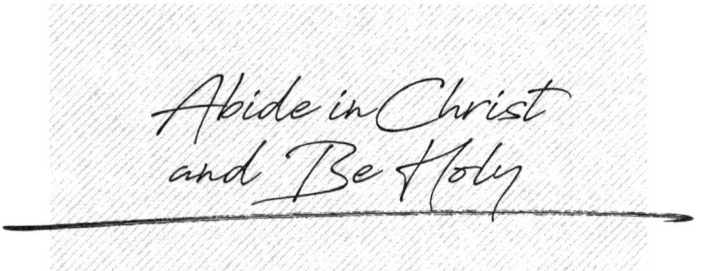

Abide in Christ and Be Holy

"I am the vine, you are the branches. He who
abides in Me, and I in him, bears much fruit;
for without Me you can do nothing."

John 15:5

I f Christians had an eve on a reigning, losing,
coming Savior, how different they would he!
What manner of person ought you to he in all
holy conversations and godliness.

How much covetousness there is among some Christians, who call money their own and clamor to acquire more luxuries. How much bitterness there is among some Christians, who have a proud and unforgiving spirit that holds grudges and nurses their anger. How much apathy there is among some Christians, who show little true love and concern for the lost.

Why is all this? Because these Christians know so little about Christ. Despite all the time Christ has been with them, they still know almost nothing about Him. Dear Christian, do not let this year go by without resolving to know more about Christ. He is still with you. Walk in the light while you have the light. Know Christ, and then you will be like Him.

Reflection

What can you do in
the coming weeks to
know Christ better?

How might you
better keep Christ
continually in your
thoughts?

Satan's Great Aim

> "Be sober, be vigilant; because your adversary
> the devil walks about like a roaring lion,
> seeking whom he may devour."
>
> *1 Peter 5:8*

Since the world's beginning, Satan's great aim has been to separate believers from the love of Christ. Although he has never succeeded in the case of a single soul, yet he still tries it as eagerly as he did at first. The moment he sees the Savior lift a lost sheep on His shoulder, from that hour he applies all his efforts to pluck the poor saved sheep from its place of rest. The moment Jesus lays His pierced hand on a poor, trembling, guilty sinner, from that hour Satan tries to pluck him out of Jesus' hand.

Satan did this in ancient times. As it is written, "For Your sake we are killed all day long; we are accounted as sheep for the slaughter" (Ps. 44:22). This is a cry taken from the book of Psalms. God's people in all ages have been hated and persecuted by Satan and the world. Why? "For Your sake"—because they were like Jesus and belonged to Jesus.

We are miserably deceived if we flatter ourselves that this same cry will not be heard again. Has the Devil changed? Does he love Christ and His dear people any better? Has the worldly heart changed? Does it hate God and God's people any less than it did? No. I have a deep conviction that if God withdrew His restraining grace, the floodgates of persecution would soon break loose again.

Reflection

Why is it so important for the church to disciple new believers, to help them become thoroughly rooted in God's truth?

In what ways has Satan tried to derail your faith in God and His Word?

The Spirit Shakes Us from Apathy

"I will pour water on him who is thirsty, and floods on the dry ground; I will pour My Spirit on your descendants, and My blessing on your offspring; they will spring up among the grass like willows by the watercourses."

Isaiah 44:3-4

There is nothing more distressing in our day than the want of growth among the children of God. They do not seem to press forward; they do not seem to be running a race. When I compare this year with last year, alas, where is the difference? There are the same weaknesses, the same coldness; no, I fear, greater languor concerning divine things.

How different things are when the Spirit is poured out! Then children of God will be like willows. You have seen the willow, how it is always growing, day or night, ever growing, ever shooting out new branches. If you cut it down, it springs up again. So would you, dear Christians, if there were a flood-time of the Holy Spirit, a day of Pentecost. Then there would be less care about your business and your workshop, more love of prayer and sweet praises. There would be more change in your heart and victory over the world, the Devil, and the flesh. You would come out and he separate. During affliction, you would grow in sweet submission, humility, and weakness.

There was a time when Sabbath-days were growing days. Hungry souls came to the Word and went away filled with good things. They came like Martha, and went away like Mary. They came like Samson when his locks were shorn and went away like Samson when his locks had grown. This day, try and give all to God.

216

Reflection

What do you think keeps many Christians from growing spiritually, from becoming like willows?

What, in your life, may be hindering your spiritual growth?

If you truly desire to grow spiritually, take time right now to talk with God and ask for His blessing and Holy Spirit infilling.

Prayer: Paul's Key to Perseverance

> "Concerning this thing [thorn in the flesh] I pleaded with the Lord three times that it might depart from me. And He said to me, 'My grace is sufficient for you, for My strength is made perfect in weakness.'"
>
> *2 Corinthians 12:8-9*

Here's the difference between a natural man and a child of God. Both have the thorn in the flesh, but a natural man is contented with it. His lusts do not vex and trouble him. A child of God cannot rest under the power of temptation. He flies to his knees. The moment Paul felt the buffetings of Satan's messenger, be fell to his knees, praying that his Father would take it away from him. No answer came. Again he went to the throne of grace. Again no answer. A third time he fell to his knees and would not let God go without a blessing.

The answer came: "My grace is sufficient for you." Not the thing Paul asked. He had asked, "Take this thorn away." God did not pluck it out of his flesh, did not drive Satan's messenger back to bell. He could have done this, but he didn't. He opened His own bosom and said, "Look here, it has pleased the Father that in Me should all fullness dwell. 'My grace is sufficient for you.'" Here is the Holy Spirit for every need of your soul. Oh, what a supply did Paul then see in Christ!

Has temptation driven you to your knees? Oh, tempted

soul, be steadfast; accept no denial. Men ought always to pray and not faint. God may not pluck out the thorn. This is a world of thorns. But look into Christ. There is enough in Him to keep your soul. The ocean is full of drops, but Christs bosom is more full of grace. Oh, pray either that your lusts may he taken away or that you may believe the grace that is in Christ Jesus.

Reflection

How do you respond to temptation?

Why is prayer so important during times of temptation?

Learn to receive God's grace and to trust in His will for you.

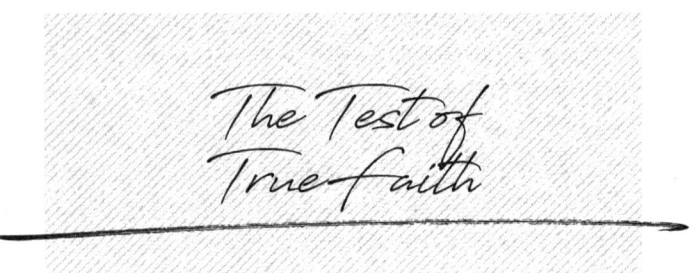

The Test of True faith

"My God, My God, why have You forsaken Me?"

Matthew 27:46

These words show the greatest faith that ever was in this world. Faith is believing the word of God, not because we see it to be true, or feel it to be true, but because God has said it. Now Christ was forsaken. He did not see that God was His God; He did not feel that God was His God. Yet He believed God's word and cried, "My God, My God."

David also shows great faith in Psalm 42:7-8: "Deep calls unto deep at the noise of Your waterfalls; all Your waves and billows have gone over me. The Lord will command His lovingkindness in the daytime, and in the night His song shall be with me—a prayer to the God of my life." He can see no light, no way of escape. Yet he believes the word of God and says, "The Lord will." This is true faith: believing when we do not see.

Reflection

In which areas is your faith being tested?

What helps you maintain faith in God even when you don't see evidence of His presence and involvement?

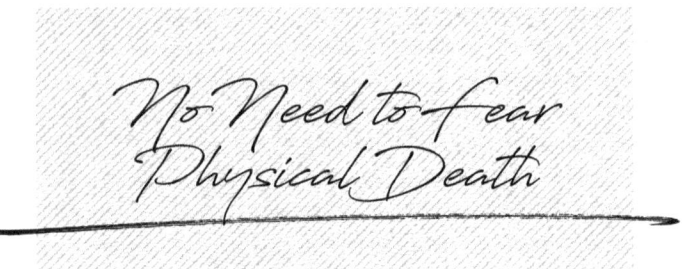

No Need to Fear Physical Death

"O Death, where is your sting? O Hades,
where is your victory? . . . Thanks be to God,
who gives us the victory through our Lord
Jesus Christ."

1 Corinthians 15:55, 57

Once you lived without prayer—without God, without Christ—in the world. Didn't Christ stretch out His hands all day long? Once you were lying under conviction of sin. Didn't Christ draw near to your soul, saying, "Peace be unto you"? Again, you w'ere groaning under temptation's power, crying out against indwelling sin: "O wretched man that I am! Who will deliver me from this body of death?" (Rom. 7:24). Didn't Christ draw near and say, "My grace is sufficient for you, for My strength is made perfect in weakness"? (2 Cor. 12:9).

Once more you may yet groan under the weight of dying agonies. The last enemy is death. It may be a hard struggle; it may be a dark valley. Yet Jesus is standing at the right hand of God, waiting to receive you to Himself. Death loses its sting when God is with you, the Spirit is within you, and Christ is waiting to receive you. Behold, He stretches out His hands to receive your departing spirit. Breathe it into His hand, saying, "Lord Jesus, receive my spirit."

Learn that death is no death to the Christian. "Whoever lives and believes in Me shall never die" (John 11:26). It is only giving the soul into the hand of Christ. He knows its value; He died for it. Learn that to die is, to the believer, better than to live. If Christ rises up to receive the soul, the soul goes to be with Jesus. But to be with Christ is to be in glory. Therefore, it is far better.

Reflection

What is the hope that all believers have concerning physical death?

How, in contrast, do many people who do not know Jesus view death?

The Spirit: Unseen, but Unfailing

"The wind blows where it wishes, and you
hear the sound of it, but cannot tell where it
comes from and where it goes. So is everyone
who is born of the Spirit."

John 3:8

Y ou do not see the wind, nor do you understand the forces and conditions that cause it to blow. Yet you spread the sail to catch the breeze, and so the tall vessel is borne over many rough seas to the haven of rest. Just so, lean on the Holy Spirit, although you don't understand His working. Although now you don't see Him, yet believe in Him and you will rejoice with joy unspeakable and full of glory. You will he home over the rough waves of this world to the haven of rest. Depend on the unseen supply of the Holy Spirit. Receive a daily supply for daily wants. Go confidently to the wells of salvation, and you will draw water with joy.

Reflection

Are you dependent on the Holy Spirit's power or trying to do most things on your own?

In what ways does the Holy Spirit's presence influence your day-to-day spiritual walk?

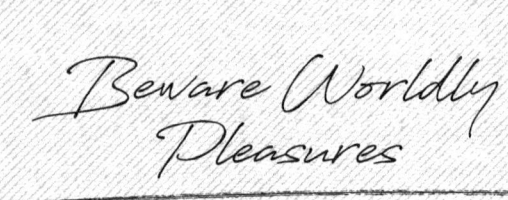
Beware Worldly Pleasures

"The ones that fell among thorns are those who, when they have heard, go out and are choked with cares, riches, and pleasures of life, and bring no fruit to maturity."

Luke 8:14

There is no net by which the Devil catches more souls than the silken one of worldly pleasure. It is common for worldly people to assume there is no harm in these things. Children are fond of games; coarser spirits love the glass, glee, and debauchery; more polished circles love the ball, concert, and play. Where is the harm? Sit down on a grave and ask the dead. Are not your days numbered?

Recall the words of Solomon: "Rejoice . . . in your youth, and let your heart cheer you in the days of your youth; walk in the ways of your heart, and in the sight of your eyes; but know that for all these God will bring you into judgment" (Eccl. 11:9).

Later, Paul wrote to Timothy: "She who lives in pleasure is dead while she lives" (1 Tim. 5:6). Are we to have no pleasure, then? Yes, in Christ—holy pleasures such as are at God's right hand forevermore. Ah, I have tasted all the pleasures of time, and they are not worth one drop of Christs sweet love.

Reflection

Which sinful pleasures tempt you?

Why is it easy to rationalize "a little sin" once in a while?

What effect has sin had on your spiritual growth?

On the lives of other people you know?

Heavenly Reward

"Then came the first [servant], saying,
'Master, your mina has earned ten minas.'
And he said to him, 'Well done, good servant;
because you were faithful in a very little, have
authority over ten cities.'"

Luke 19:16-17

E very man will be rewarded according to how his work has been. Some will he made rulers over five cities, some over ten cities. I have no doubt that even sin, inconsistency, back-sliding. and decay of God's children take away something from their eternal glory. It is a loss for all eternity.

The more fully and unreservedly we follow the Lord Jesus now, the more abundant will our entrance he into His everlasting kingdom. The closer we walk with Christ now, the closer we will walk with Him through all eternity. "You have a few names even in Sardis who have not defiled their garments; and they shall walk with Me in white, for they are worthy" (Rev. 3:4).

Reflection

When you think about heaven, do you think about the rewards God will give to His faithful people?

Why or why not?

How might you live differently if you keep this truth in mind?

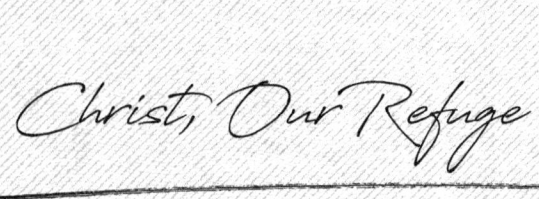

Christ, Our Refuge

"Come, my people, enter your chambers, and
shut your doors behind you; hide yourself, as
it were, for a little moment, until the
indignation is past."

Isaiah 26:20

C hrist is like our own chamber with the door
shut, in many respects.

There is safety in Him. There is no place in
all the world to which we look more often in an hour of
danger, as a refuge and place of safety, than our own
home—the inner chamber with the door locked. Likewise,
brethren, there is safety in Christ. "There is therefore
now no condemnation to those who are in Christ Jesus"
(Rom. 8:1).

There is quietness and rest in Him. In the world, we
look for the bustle and harassment of business. But when
we enter our chamber and shut the door behind us, we
shut out the bustling, noisy world; all is tranquility and
peace. Brethren, such is Christ. In Him, the "weary are
at rest." We have quietness and assurance forever.

Our home is a ready-made retreat, near and easy of access.
When we seek our home, we don't have to soar with the
eagle to the top of the rugged rocks or be like the dove
that nests in the hole's mouth. Neither must we dig into
the earth so that we may hide our head there. Our home

is near us. Just such is Christ. He is a ready-made Savior, at hand and not far off. This is the all-sufficient refuge that God bids His people to flee into during every storm.

Reflection

When you experience difficulties and uncertainties, how quickly do you turn to Jesus?

How does He promise to respond when you turn to Him?

Are You Thirsty for God?

"Everyone who thirsts, come to the waters . .
. and let your soul delight itself in
abundance."

Isaiah 55:1-2

W hat do "thirsty believers" look like? How do we know they are thirsting for God and His satisfying waters? Two signs immediately become clear: They thirst after God's Word and they thirst after communion with God through prayer.

When two travelers are going through the wilderness, you may know which of them is thirsty the way he is always looking for wells. How gladly Israel came to Him, where there were twelve wells of water and seventy' palm trees! So it is with thirsty believers. They love the Word, read and preached. They thirst for it more and more.

And so it is with prayer also. When a little child is thirsty for its mother's breast, it will not keep silent, nor will a child ol God who is thirsty. Thirst will lead you to the secret well where you may draw unseen the living water. It will lead you to united prayer. If the town were in want of water, and thirst staring every man in the face, would you not meet one with another, consult, and help to dig new wells? Now the town is in need of grace, souls are perishing for lack of it, and you are languishing.

Oh, meet to pray. "If two of you agree on earth concerning anything that they ask, it will he done for them by My Father in heaven" (Matt. 18:19).

Reflection

Why is prayer as the body of Christ so important?

If we are not spiritually thirsts; how do we rekindle such desire for the Bible and prayer?

What are some of the ways in which the "world" tries to satisfy our thirst?

Take Joy in What's to Come

"He has reconciled in the body of His flesh
through death, to present you holy, and
blameless, and above reproach in His sight."

Colossians 1:21-22

I n that day, Christ will take those of you whom He has redeemed and reconciled, and present you to Himself a glorious church. He wall confess your name before His Father and present you faultless before the presence of His glory with exceeding joy. Saints will have a double perfection in that day.

You will be perfectly righteous. You will be "unreprovable." Satan will accuse you; Christ will show His scars and say, "I died for that soul."

You will be perfectly holy. You will leave the body of sin behind you. The Spirit who dwells in you now will complete His work. You will be like Jesus, for you will see Him as He is. You will be holy as God is holy, pure as Christ is pure.

If Christ has truly begun a good work in you, He will perform it until the day of Christ Jesus. Christ says, "I am the Alpha and the Omega, the Beginning and the End" (Rev. 1:8). Whenever He begins, He will make an end. Whenever He builds a stone as the foundation, He will preserve it unshaken until the end. Only make sure that you are upon the foundation, that you are reconciled, that you have true peace with God. Then you may look across the mountains and rivers that are between you and that day, and say, "He is able to keep me from falling." You have but two shallow brooks to pass through—sickness and death—and He has promised to meet you, to go with you, foot by foot. A few more tears, a few more temptations, a few more agonizing prayers, a few more sacraments, and you will stand with the Lamb on Mount Zion!

Reflection

Do you look forward to heaven? Why do some Christians seem not to anticipate going to heaven? Why is it important to always remember that we believers are citizens of heaven, not citizens of earth?

Be Steadfast in the faith

"Continue in the faith, grounded and steadfast."

Colossians 1:23

D ear believers, see that you continue in the faith. Remember, you will be tried.

You may be tried by false doctrine. Satan may change himself into an angel of light and try to beguile you by another gospel. "Hold fast the pattern of sound words" (2 Tim. 1:13).

You will be tried by persecution. The world will hate you for your love of Christ. They will speak all manner of evil against you falsely.

You will be tried by flattery. The world will smile on you. Satan will spread his paths with flowers; he will perfume his bed with myrrh, aloes, and cinnamon.

Can you withstand all these enemies? Perseverance is essential to salvation, as essential as faith or as the new birth. True, everyone who believes in Christ will be saved, but they will be saved through perseverance. "If anyone does not abide in Me, he is cast out as a branch and is withered; and they gather them and throw them into the fire, and they are burned" (John 15:6). Behold, in Jesus there is strength for perseverance.

Reflection

What does the word
perseverance mean?

In what way(s) are
you lacking
perseverance in the
faith?

Which temptations
do you find most
appealing?

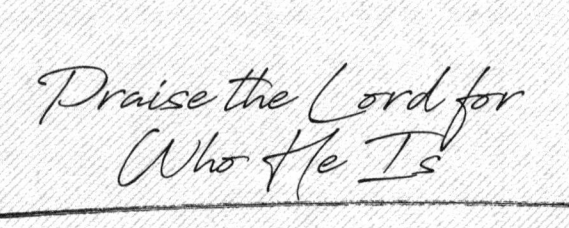
Praise the Lord for Who He Is

"Praise the Lord with the harp, make melody
to Him with an instrument of ten strings.
Sing to Him a new song; play skillfully with a
shout of joy."

Psalm 33:2-3

An unconverted man sees no loveliness in God. He sees beauty in the blue sky, glorious sun, green earth, spangling stars, and lily of the field, but he sees no beauty in God. This man has not seen Him, nor known Him, therefore there is no melody of praise in that heart.

When a sinner is brought to Christ, he is brought to the Father. Jesus gave Himself for us that He might bring us to God. Oh. what a sight breaks in on the soul—the infinite, eternal, unchangeable God! I know some of you have been brought to see this sight. Praise Him, then, for who He is. Praise Him for His pure, lovely holiness that cannot bear any sin in His sight. Cry, like the angels, "Holy, holy, holy, Lord God Almighty" (Rev. 4:8). Praise Him for His infinite wisdom; He knows the end from the beginning. In Him are hidden all the treasures of wisdom and knowledge. Praise Him for His power; all matter, all mind, is in His hand. The heart of the king, the heart of saint and sinner, are all in His hand. Hallelujah, for the Lord God omnipotent reigns.

Praise Him for His love, for God is love. Some of you

have been at sea. When far out of sight of land, you have stood high on the vessel's prow and looked around and around, one vast circle without any boundary. Oh, so it is to stand in Christ, justified, and to behold the love of God, a vast ocean all around you, without a bottom and without a shore. Oh, praise Him for Who He is.

Reflection

For which attributes of God are you most thankful? Set aside time today to praise God for who He is and what He has done in your life.

Give God the Honor Due Him

"God has sent His only begotten Son into the
world, that we might live through Him. In
this is love, not that we loved God, but that
He loved us and sent His Son to be the
propitiation for our sins."

1 John 4:9-10

G od spared not His own Son. Herein is love.
He loved the happiness of His Son, but He
loved the salvation of sinners more. He loved
to have His Son in His bosom, but He loved more to have
sinners brought into His bosom, fie east out His Son in
order to take us in. Sinner, how will you escape if you
neglect so great a salvation?

Learn that God must have the glory of this. He wall
not give His glory to another. Some view God as an
angry, inexorable judge but view Christ as a smiling
Savior who comes between us and an angry Father. You
will never come to peace as long as you think this. This
is robbing God of His glory. God wishes you to honor
the Son even as you honor the Father, but not more than
you honor the Father. You will never come to peace until
you look to Christ as the gift of God, until you see that
the heart of God and Christ are one in this matter, until
God shows you the love that provided, upheld, and gave
up the Son.

Reflection

What is your view
of God the Father?

How has it affected
your relationship
with Him?

In what ways do
people fail to give
God the glory?

Faith in Action

"Faith by itself, if it does not have works, is dead."

James 2:17

M any Christians are content to be Christians for themselves: to hug the gospel to themselves, to sit in their own rooms and feast upon it alone. Christ didn't do this. It is true that He loved to he alone. He once said to His disciples, "Come aside by yourselves to a deserted place and rest a while" (Mark 6:31). He often spent the night in prayer on the lone mountainside, but also He traveled continually. He went and saw, then He had compassion. He didn't hide Himself from other people.

You should be Christlike. Your word should be, "Go and see." Go and see the poor, and then you will feel for them. Remember what Jesus said to all His people: "I was sick and you visited Me; I was in prison and you came to Me" (Matt. 25:36).

Don't be deceived, my dear friends. It is easy to give a cold pittance of charity at the church door and to think that that is the religion of Jesus. But, "Pure and undefiled religion before God and the Father is this: to visit orphans and widows in their trouble, and to keep oneself unspotted from the world" (James 1:27).

Christ had compassion on the multitudes, and will you have none? Christ gave Himself for them; what will you give?

Reflection

Which persons might you "go and see" soon?
What happens to our faith if it is not put into action?

Rely on God's Strength, Not Your Own

"My grace is sufficient for you, for My strength is made perfect in weakness."

2 Corinthians 12:9

W hen you trust in Jesus for strength, you must feel that your own resolutions, vows, and promises are as useless to stem the current of your passions as so many straws would be in stemming the mightiest waterfall. You must feel that your own earnestness and strength of disposition, which has so long been the praise of your friends and the boast of your mind, are as powerless before the breath of temptation as a broken reed before the hurricane. You must feel that you wrestle not with flesh and blood, but with spirits of gigantic power in whose mighty grasp you are feeble as a child. Then, and only then, will you come with all your heart to trust in the Lord your strength.

When the believer is weakest, he is strongest. The child who knows most its utter feebleness entrusts itself most completely into the mother's arms. The young eagle that knows, by many a fall, its own inability to fly yields itself to be carried on the mother's mighty wing. When it is weak, it is strong. Likewise, the believer, when he has found out, by repeated falls, his utter feebleness, clings with simplest faith to the arm of the Savior.

Reflection

Do you really believe this truth?

Or are you still, subtly or secretly, trying to face temptations on your own, in your strength?

You Have Been Pardoned

A soul in Christ is a pardoned soul. It matters not how many sins he has committed. The iniquity of Jerusalem was very great. Its people had sinned against light and against love. All the prophets sent to them were stoned or killed. The Son of God came there; they cast Him out of the vineyard and killed Him! Their sins had grown up to heaven; yet no sooner do they turn to Christ than God says, "Her iniquity is pardoned" (Isa. 40:2). And, observe, it is a *present* pardon. God does not say, "Her iniquity will he pardoned," but, "Her iniquity is pardoned."

No sooner does a guilty, heavy-laden soul turn to Christ than this sweet word is heard in heaven—his iniquity is pardoned. "There is therefore now no condemnation to those who are in Christ Jesus" (Rom. 8:1). It is no future or uncertain pardon that is offered in the gospel, but a sure and present pardon—pardon now, this instant, to all who believe in Jesus. You are as completely pardoned in the moment of believing as ever you will be.

It is a holy pardon. Your iniquity is pardoned; another has died for your sins. It is an awful way of pardon. It is a pardon to make you tremble and hate sin with a perfect hatred. Oh, can you ever love that which nailed Jesus to the tree, which bowed down His blessed head? Will you take up sin again, and thus put the spear afresh into His side? Some people say, "I am too vile." Are you viler than Jerusalem? When you take a pebble and cast it into the deep sea, it sinks and is entirely covered. So are the sins of those who take refuge in Christ.

Reflection

Why is it important for us to confess our sins to God?

What happens when we let them accumulate and become a burden?

And what are we communicating to God when we do not receive the forgiveness He offers?

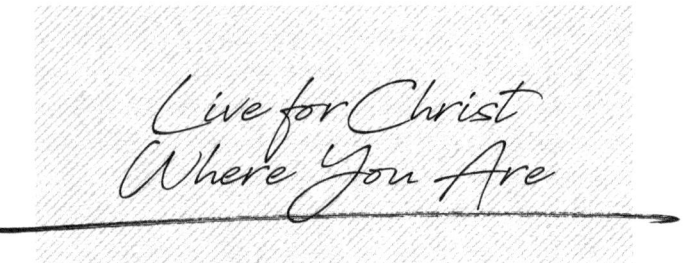

Live for Christ Where You Are

"God has set the members, each one of them, in the body just as He pleased. And if they were all one member, where would the body be?"

1 Corinthians 12:18–19

In a great house, every servant has his own peculiar work. Everyone has his proper place, and no servant interferes with another. If all were to become porters and open the door, what would become of the stewards? Or, if all were to be stewards, who would clean the house? It is the same with Christians. Everyone has his peculiar work assigned him and should not leave it. "Let each one remain in the same calling in which he was called" (1 Cor. 7:20).

Obadiah had his work appointed him in wicked Ahab's court. Do any of you belong to a wicked family? Seek not to be removed. Christ has placed you there to be His servant, so work for Him. Once a poor demoniac whom Jesus healed begged to follow after Him. Jesus did not permit him, but said to him, "Go home to your friends, and tell them what great things the Lord has done for you, and how He has had compassion on you" (Mark 5:19).

Learn, dear friends, to keep to your own work. When the Lord has hung up a lamp in one corner, is there no presumption in removing it to another? Is not the Lord wiser than man? Each of you has your work to do for Christ *where you are*. Are you on a sickbed? You still have your work to do for Christ there as much as the highest servant of Christ in the world. The smallest twinkling star is as much a servant of God as the midday sun. Only live for Christ where you are.

Reflection

Where has God placed you?
To what extent are you serving Him there?
Ask Him to give you opportunities to reflect His light and truth to others around you.

Cling Tightly to God No Matter What

"You are my strong refuge. Let my mouth be
filled with Your praise and with Your glory
all the day."

Psalm 71:7–8

The eternal God is your refuge. Of whom can
you be afraid? Remember, abide in Him. During the dark hours of sin and temptation, Satan always tries to drive you from this refuge. He will
try to make you doubt if Christ is God, if His work is a
finished work, if sinners and backsliders may find refuge
in Him. But don't throw away your confidence. Cling
tightly to God, for He is your refuge.

During the hour of death, you may have a dark valley
to pass through. You may lose sight of all your evidences.
You may feel all your graces leave and cry, "All these
things are against me." Still, as a helpless sinner, flee to
the Savior God. Your eyes will close on this world only
to open on the world where there is no doubt, no fear,
and no death.

Reflection

When do you tend
to doubt God?

When temptations
and difficulties
assail you, do you
find it easy to find
refuge in Him?

Why or why not?

Subject Index

Abiding with God

Adversity

Bible

Blessings of God

Body of Christ

Gospel of Christ

Grace

Holiness

Holy Spirit

Spiritual Growth

Spiritual Warfare

Strength

Suffering

Surrender to God

Worship

If you have enjoyed this book, look out for these other
additions to the series for sale online:

The Best of Andrew Murray
The Best of George MacDonald
The Best of Jonathan Edwards
The Best of F. B. Meyer
The Best of E. M. Bounds
The Best of Charles Spurgeon
The Best of D. L. Moody

If this book has impacted your life, we would love to hear
from you.
Please contact us at info@honorbooks.com